Synergies

Errata

p.xii	line 10:	McDonald *for* Macdonald
	line 32:	its students *for* their students
p.xxiii	line 10:	synonymised *for* synonimised
	line 12:	Hobsbaum *for* Habsbaum
p.xxiv	line 6:	dactylic *for* dactyllic
p.xxv	last line:	Marlowe *for* Marvell
p.26	line 4:	Leopold *for* Harold
p.60	line 28:	who fell *for* who feel
p.75	line 18:	Apokoinou *for* apo-koinu
p.90	line 17:	chiastic *for* chiasmic

SYNERGIES

Creative Writing in Academic Practice

Edited by Lucy Newlyn and Jenny Lewis

Vol. I: Sea Sonnets

The St Edmund Hall Poetry Workshop

This edition published in 2003 by
Chough Publications
St Edmund Hall
OXFORD
OX1 4AR

A catalogue record for this book is available from the British Library.

ISBN 0-954 5084-08 Paper

Cover design: 'Rough Salt History' by Lucy Wilkinson

Typesetting by Gillian Powell

Printed in the United Kingdom by The Holywell Press

Participants in St Edmund Hall Poetry Workshop

All participants are members of St Edmund Hall, Oxford. The workshops were led by Jenny Lewis and Lucy Newlyn.

Jenny Lewis, Freelance writer; Creative Writing Tutor (poetry), the University of Oxford Creative Writing Diploma.

Dr. Lucy Newlyn, Fellow and Tutor in English, St Edmund Hall

Caroline Boon, Third Year English

Ben Burton, Third Year English

Charlene Dy, Visiting Student, Year Abroad Programme, 2001-2

Daniel Harkin, Second Year English

Brendan Jones, Fourth Year English and Modern Languages

Elizabeth Scott-Baumann, Third Year English

Alice Wood, Second Year English

Observer and Commentator

Paul Ashwin, Institute for the Advancement of University Learning, The University of Oxford.

Acknowledgements

Our thanks, first and foremost, to the participants in our workshops for their tireless enthusiasm, and the ungrudging use of time they might have spent on other things.

We are very grateful indeed to Paul Ashwin, of the Institute for the Advancement of University Learning, for his encouragement of this project and for agreeing to write an article about it, which appears at the end of this book. Our thanks also to the Institute for the Advancement of University Learning, who have funded the publication of our findings in book form; and to Jane Griffiths, who commented on a final draft of this volume. Gill Powell has kindly converted our document into camera-ready copy.

L.N. and J.L.

Table of Contents

Preface

by Jenny Lewis

In an article published in *The Observer* in 1982, John Rae, the Headmaster of Westminster School, condemned the teaching of creative writing, linking it to 'the decline of grammar' and the demise of social qualities such as 'honesty, responsibility, gratitude, apology and so on'. This mistrust seems odd, given that Shakespeare was a creative writer, as, in their day, were all the writers in the Western canon.

Seven years later, in 1989, the Cox Report (*The Importance of English in the Curriculum*), was far more tolerant of change and accepted the premise that literary and non-literary writing could have a beneficial cross-over effect on one another. In fact, Professor Cox went as far as to say that opportunities for writing as part of a pupil's cognitive development should flourish because writing, including creative writing, is central to an individual's 'ability to communicate effectively with the outside world'.

Since the 1990's the status of creative writing has steadily advanced, especially in the States, where it is seen as a 'growth point', not only for attracting students, 'but in the original meaning of the phrase, the place where the cells are actively dividing.' Not surprisingly, in North American Universities, cutting edge creative writing tuition holds a key position in the academic curriculum, and includes collaborative or associative writing linked by computers, to give the potential of powerful communal video and sound applications (such as installations) and other benefits of technology. As daily progress is made on the other side of the Atlantic, it seems odd and backward that some British institutions are still balking at the idea of including creative writing in their syllabus at all.

While the aftermath of the Bullock Report still lingers in many academic institutions, especially traditional ones like Oxford and Cambridge, a major new government initiative is funding research into the importance of creativity as a vital part of the learning process. In the Guardian Education section of 9 September 2002, Peter Jenkinson announced the investment of £40 million by the Department of Culture, Media and Sport (working closely with the Department of Education) in new programmes which link creative activity into the curriculum and aspirations of schools. Jenkinson, the National Director of Creative Partnerships (the Arts Council body developing these programmes) explained why there is a crucial need, in the development of children and young people, to enhance creativity in the learning process. In his eyes

> Reconnecting with the innate skills of creativity – of being an excellent communicator, of being able to generate new ideas, to work as a team, to take risks, to solve problems – will lead to…a workforce more attuned to the requirements of 21st century society.

As Jenkinson says, too many children and young people go into adulthood with 'stifled creativity' meaning they are 'ill equipped to realise their full potential either as individuals or as active citizens in their communities'. Projects already set up include associations with art galleries, artists, theatres, musicians, poets and dramatists in a bid to inspire and encourage young people and those that teach and care for them, to 'transform expectations' and to stimulate 'innovative thinking' throughout the education system.

The importance given to Creative Writing as a key element of the American system is born out by the fact that Paul Muldoon, Professor of Poetry at Oxford University, is concurrently Director of the Creative Writing programme at Princeton University. He has also taught Creative Writing at the universities of Columbia, Berkeley and Massachusetts. In an interview for the Oxford University Gazette, 20 May 1999, Professor Muldoon said 'I firmly believe there is no distinction between creative and critical writing, and am looking forward to exploring a wide range of aspects of poetry in English'. Although some might find it hard to agree that there is no distinction between the critical and the creative, the fact that Professor Muldoon gives them equal weight may help to dispel the myth that the creative is in any way inferior to the critical in the exploration and analysis of English.

In May 2001, *The Guardian* published an article by Claire Armistead, Literary Editor of *The Guardian* (who read English at Oxford). The article was headed 'University Guide: Creative Writing is on the increase'. Warwick University and its Creative Writing MA had moved into the number one spot by virtue of a combination of a 'firmly structured curriculum and a strong cultural life, based on a thriving arts centre'. In summer 2002, Warwick held a symposium at which one of the subjects was 'Creative Writing as an academic subject'. Another university which scored highly for its combination of Creative Writing with academic teaching was Glamorgan. Sussex University runs an MA in Creative and Critical Writing which is based on the premise that 'theory' and 'practice' are not opposites, and that the critical and the creative are 'necessarily intertwined'. In September 2000, Newcastle University set up a seven week module where medical students could write poetry and fiction alongside completing their medical curriculum. Newcastle's Professor of Epidemiology and Public Health, Richard Thompson, said

> It's partly about students being able to express themselves well and partly about the therapeutic components of creative writing...but it's also about meeting the need for a wider education of doctors.

Carol Clewlow, the Medical School's first Writer in Residence, said she wanted to help medical students to use writing therapeutically in order to understand and express their expectations and fears about becoming doctors, and to 'use literature as a resource for learning about people'.

While an increasing number of British universities are recognising the validity of Creative Writing and adding it to their curriculi, it is hard to forget that as recently as 1999, OUP axed its contemporary poetry list. The reason given was that Oxford is an academic institution which is ill-placed to publish and market contemporary poetry and fiction. Sir Keith Thomas commented that OUP, by being guardians of the OED, were acting as custodians of the English Language. Alan Howarth, the Minister of Culture, condemned the decision as 'barbaric' and commented in *The Oxford Magazine* that

> ...poets no less than lexicographers are shapers of the English language. The custodian is abandoning its task if it abandons our poets.

A frequently heard comment from academics is that contemporary writing, especially poetry, rather than being included on the syllabus, can be adequately enjoyed through poetry readings, reading groups and poetry societies. This is true, although the number of English undergraduates who belong to and/or turn up to readings organised by the Oxford University Poetry Society is shamefully small. Many colleges have their own poetry societies, and Peter MacDonald runs poetry classes and workshops for undergraduates reading English. The OUPS's magazine, *The Reader,* is published termly and is one outlet for student work. Another new one is *The Ladder.*

There are plenty of opportunities to hear poetry read in Oxford. Groups such as Poetic Licence used to meet at the Jericho Café for readings by poets followed by open mic sessions. Their events now are a more moveable feast. Their offshoot, Poetic off-Licence, runs unique wine and poetry-tasting events for the Oxford Literary Festival. The Oxford Literary Festival, which runs in April, usually includes several poetry events as part of its inspired literary and cultural mix. Oxford Brookes University appoints regular Poets in Residence (recently, the Nigerian poet Patience Agbabe); and has a thriving contemporary poetry life. There are also well publicised poetry events as part of the International Women's Festival (in March) and on National Poetry Day (October).

For those who want to write themselves and to find support systems, Backroom Poets, run by the indefatigable Rip Bulkeley, organises a programme of readings by well known and lesser known poets, workshops at members' houses, and regular readings at Borders Bookshop where members can try out their poems on passers by. Marcus Moore and Mary Jane Arbury run popular Poetry Slams at the Playhouse in Oxford (as well as at several other venues, including in London). Stanford University organises Creative Writing tutorials for their students at Oxford University, and the Oxford University Department of Continuing Education runs a two-year Creative Writing Diploma of which Poetry is an essential element.

Added to this, there are many Creative Writing books available. *Becoming a Writer* by Dorothea Brande, published in 1934 by Harcourt Brace and Co., with a forward by John Braine, has never been bettered for rational yet sympathetic advice for aspiring writers. *Writing Down the Bones,* by Natalie Goldberg (Shambhala, 1986) is a more New Age approach. Andrew Motion has published a weighty volume extolling the methods of the world-renowned UEA Creative Writing course. Mark Strand and Eavan Boland's *The Making of a Poem* (W.W. Norton & Co, 2000) is an excellent guide to different forms, and poets such as Don Paterson, Ruth Padel and Matthew Sweeney have all written 'How To' poetry books of one sort or another.

On the other hand are the critically biased books such as *The Poetry Handbook: a guide to reading Poetry for Pleasure and Criticism* by John Lennard (OUP 1996), and *An Introduction to English Poetry* by James Fenton (Viking 2002) which explores form from a traditional standpoint. What seems to be missing is any sort of meeting place between Creative Writing and Critical Commentary that can be accessed on a regular basis by undergraduates through an interactive process in which the creative and the critical are encouraged to enhance one another.

In the same issue of the Oxford Magazine that included Alan Howarth's 'barbarians' speech, Karen Leeder, Fellow in German at New College, said that '...once mobilised, poetry possesses extraordinary, often unsuspected energies'. It's these energies we need to tap into to create future generations of graduates who can look to a future where their creative and critical abilities have been equally developed in order to give them more hope of a balanced working life.

Introduction
by Lucy Newlyn

Creative writers may have highly developed critical faculties, which they exercise intuitively, or apply with varying degrees of awareness, in the process of creation. Most critics, on the other hand, are not 'creative', except in a secondary sense. They may know, at a very sophisticated level, how a sonnet is made, but they do not usually make sonnets themselves. Critical analysis (otherwise known as close reading) as it has been taught at Oxford University, is indeed a purely academic exercise. Elsewhere, too, students are taught the art of writing *about* literature; and as a separate exercise they may also be encouraged in, or taught, 'creative writing'. But these two disciplines are seldom approached in tandem.

Over the last two years at St Edmund Hall, Jenny Lewis and I have been experimenting with a method designed to harness together the creative and critical faculties. We began from the following shared premises:

1. The academic study of English is potentially creative.
2. Literary studies can be improved by a degree of practical know-how: in other words, by learning and applying the 'craft' of writing.
3. Creative writing is enhanced by critical awareness.
4. The synergy of creative writing and critical writing is something to be fostered in teachers and students alike.

We arrived at these premises independently and by very different routes. Jenny Lewis is primarily a creative writer: she has been publishing poetry, children's books, and plays over a period of twenty years. She has also for many years taught creative writing, but not in an academic fashion. She studied literature as an academic subject relatively late in life, successfully completing her Oxford degree (as a mature student) in 2000. I have for twenty years taught and written about English literature; and my three published books are works of criticism. Only three years ago did I start writing my own poetry, which I have now begun to publish.

Both of us had experienced at first hand the deepening and enriching of our capacities as readers and writers, which came about by crossing the creative/critical divide, each in a different direction. We wanted to see if we could encourage a similar experience in others. We did this over a year or so, with dramatic results among undergraduates reading English at St Edmund Hall. Not only did our teaching method result in enjoyable and stimulating workshops; it also produced better essays from the undergraduates, and some good poetry. The most important product of all was a happier, more purposeful group of students, who felt that their creative identities were valued. There was a consequent increase in the level of their commitment to academic study, a better group dynamic in college classes, and a consciously articulated sense of confidence and empowerment on the part of students and teachers alike. Ben Burton, one of our undergraduate participants, commented:

> Poetry workshops have proved an exciting and valuable part of Teddy Hall's English course. The roles of Tutor and student are forgotten, as all participate equally in the creative process, both in producing collective pieces and in sharing their individual work. In this way, workshop members have been able to discover and embrace their differences.

Our experience of workshop writing, and of its benefits in academic practice, has encouraged us to pass on our findings to others. Thanks to a generous grant from the Institute for the Advancement of University Learning, we have been able to publish our findings in the form of a two-volume book. This, the first volume, is intended partly as a teaching-manual and study-guide, partly as a research archive. In it, we have recorded, stage by stage, the method we have been adopting. We have also included the work produced by participants in the process, together with feedback on completion of the experiment and an essay on the implications of our methodology for the teaching of English. The second volume is designed more as an anthology than as a manual: it ranges widely over a number of different forms, demonstrating a variety of ways in which creative writing can be encouraged and integrated into academic study.

A New Teaching-Model

Our method involved a six-stage process of creative and critical writing. Jenny and I began by choosing a topic (the sea) and a form (the sonnet) which we would be focusing on for subsequent workshops. Each workshop represented a discrete stage in the process of harnessing critical analysis and creative writing. A record was kept of every stage, and these were collected at the end.

Stage One: Collaborative Writing

At our first workshop, Jenny and I announced that the sea and the sonnet-form were to provide a focus for thinking and writing. We began by discussing the sonnet as a form, looking at examples of Shakespearean and Petrarchan sonnets, noting their different rhyme-schemes etc. This part of the workshop resembled a standard academic class. (For further information about the sonnet as a form, see glossary below).

Then we turned to creative writing. In advance, we had selected a number of key words, known as 'trigger words', which were designed to provoke associations. In response to these trigger words (which Jenny read aloud), each member of the group wrote down ideas, words, images. These were then read aloud by each member of the group. Collaboratively, the group then selected the 'best' (most evocative, unusual, striking, original) words from each person's list, and these made a composite pool of words, from which it was hoped that a poem would grow. (Already, critical judgements had been involved and explained by each person to the group, and a kind of critical consensus had been reached through selection and discussion).

Jenny Lewis, on behalf of the group, then produced a finished version of the edited group poem, simply by typing up all the words in the order of the writers, and putting each participant's selected words on a new line.

Stage Two: Individual Writing

All members of the group worked independently on their own poems, using words from the group pool as much as possible, so as to preserve the collaborative quality of the poetry. They returned to the next workshop with their finished poems, which were read aloud and discussed. Printed copies of the poems were then circulated in time for the next workshop. Each member of the group wrote a short account of their own poem: what they intended to achieve and how. (At this stage, they were being asked to reflect critically on their own creative processes. They were learning to apply to their own work an academic skill which they would usually apply to the work of others). Group members did not circulate these personal accounts of their poems, but they did bring them along to the next workshop.

Stage Three: Collaborative Criticism

Each person arrived prepared to criticise all the poems produced, including their own. A group discussion of each poem followed; and each contributor explained to the group what they intended to do in their own poems, after they had heard the group's reaction to their work. At this stage, a kind of friction developed between what the author 'intended' in their poem, and how the readers (individually and collectively) interpreted it. This proved an extremely fruitful area for discussion and theoretical reflection. For students interested in reader-response and hermeneutics, it provided a practical, hands-on, method of testing out ideas they had been learning to explore more theoretically in other parts of their course. Ben Burton comments:

> I have always supported the theory that an author's intention can never be fully known from a text, but felt rather squeamish when I discovered how this theory affected the reception of my own poem. Could other readers share in the meaning I had spent so long in developing in my poem, or was it inevitable that each would discover their own interpretation? I think I will be spending a little longer mourning 'the death of the author'.

Stage Four: Individual Criticism

All members of the group were divided into pairs. Each person wrote a commentary on their partner's poem. These commentaries were circulated, and discussion of the critical analysis followed in a subsequent workshop.

Stage Five: Editing to make a new poem

Each member of the group took his or her partner's poem and reduced it to a pool of words and ideas which provided a jumping off point for the reader's own associations. A new poem was created from the 'wreckage' of the original. This stage of the process allowed exploration of concepts such as the 'death of the author' and reader response theory. Cut text, and comparisons with its original body, are the subject of experiments by such contemporary poets as Selima Hill.

Stage Six: Feed Back

The last stage of the whole process was that each member of the experiment looked back on it, and reflected on what worked for them and what didn't, what they found surprising and/or useful, etc.

How to use this book

Readers interested in how our methodology could help in studying/teaching elementary Critical Theory might like to turn to the final section of this book, where they will find a short essay on the subject. Those interested in the work produced in the course of our workshops should proceed directly to the next section, entitled STAGE ONE.

The workshop material is presented author-by-author, so as to show how a poem generates commentary. This should enable easy cross-reference between authorial introduction, critical analysis, and edited text.

A glossary of terms is supplied. For further reading on the sonnet form, see *The Making of a Poem*, ed. Mark Strand and Eavan Boland; *Poetry* by John Strachan and Richard Terry; *The Poetry Handbook* by John Lennard; and *The Penguin Book of the Sonnet*, ed. Phillis Levin.

Glossary of terms frequently used in this volume

Sonnet

A poem of fourteen lines, usually in *iambic pentameter* and with an intricate rhyme scheme following one of two patterns (see *Petrarchan* and *Shakespearean*, below). There are twelve-line and sixteen-line variants. The sonnet form came into the English language via Sir Thomas Wyatt and the Earl of Surrey in the early sixteenth century. It has traditionally been associated with the exploration of love; and there are several famous Elizabethan sonnet-sequences on this subject, including those by Sir Philip Sidney (*Astrophil and Stella,* 1580-3); Spenser's *Amoretti* (1595) and Shakespeare's *Sonnets* (1609). Death and religious faith are among the other themes commonly approached through the sonnet form, which appealed particularly to Donne, Wordsworth, Hopkins, Owen, and Auden.

Petrarchan (or Italian) sonnet

This sonnet-form takes its name from the fourteenth-century Italian poet, Petrarch, who used it extensively. It has an *octave* (eight lines) and a *sestet* (six lines). The rhyme scheme more commonly rhymes *ABBA ABBA CDE CDE;* although there are variants on this. (Rhyme variations in the sestet are admissible, but rhymes are limited to five). Usually the octave is used to set out a problem, while the sestet is used to resolve it.

Shakepearean (or English) sonnet

This form consists of three quatrains and a couplet. It rhymes *ABAB, CDCD, EFEF, GG*. The metre is *iambic pentameter.* The elaborate rhyme scheme signals that the poet is trying to reconcile contradictory feelings. The couplet is frequently used (as in Shakespeare) to introduce a new idea, or to tie the sonnet up neatly.

Spenserian or Sidneyan sonnet

A sonnet rhyming *ABAB, BCBC, CDCD, EE.* It is also known as the link sonnet, because of its rhyme-scheme, which links the second quatrain back into the first; and the third into the second. This form has the binding couplet at the end, as in the Shakespearean sonnet.

Miltonic Sonnet

This follows the same rhyme scheme as the Petrarchan sonnet; but the *volta* is delayed until around the tenth line, or dispensed with altogether. The rhyme scheme in the sestet is also flexible. Milton was adept at using couplets in his sonnets, but frequently avoided doing so: as a result, his sonnets end on a more open-ended note than do Shakespeare's. However, Milton's most famous sonnet is probably 'When I consider how my light is spent', which achieves a marvellous sense of closure without needing to use a couplet.

volta

A term used to describe the turning point in a sonnet where the poet shifts from one mood to another, or stands back from a problem s/he has been exploring, and tries to resolve it. This usually occurs in the Petrarchan sonnet between the eighth and ninth lines; but it can be used in other kinds of sonnet, and in different places.

enjambement

This is applied to lines in which the sense carries through from one line to the next, producing a smooth flowing effect. It is the opposite of an end-stopped line.

caesura

A pause in the line, usually occuring half-way through, and often marked by punctuation, as in the famous line from *Hamlet*: 'To be or not to be, that is the question'.

alliteration

The repeated use of the same consonants in two or more words near to each other.

half-rhyme

A half-rhyme occurs when *either* the last stressed vowels *or* the consonants that follow them (but not both) of two or more words are identical. The effect of half-rhyme is slightly dissonant and anti-climactic. It is often used to create an eerie or uncomfortable feeling in the reader. The greatest master of half-rhyme in the English language is Wilfred Owen, who frequently organised whole poems around it. (See *pararhyme*, below).

pararhyme
Strictly speaking, pararhyme is a subset of half-rhyme. It occurs when the words have the same consonantal pattern, but where the vowels vary (as in the words 'hat' and 'hot'). However – and this can be a little confusing – the term 'pararhyme' is often used to describe rhymes in which the vowels as well as the consonants relate to each other ('knive us', 'nervous'). Thus, the terms 'pararhyme' and 'half-rhyme' have gradually become more or less synonimised in general usage. For an excellent discussion of rhyme, pararhyme, half-rhyme, and even three quarter-rhyme, in the poetry of Wilfred Owen, see Philip Habsbaum's *Metre, Rhythm and Verse Form* (Routlege, 1996), p. 45-7.

feminine rhyme/ending
This is the politically incorrect term used to describe either a rhyme or a line ending, which contains one or more unstressed extra beats. The effect produced is sometimes referred to as 'weak' or 'falling'. In the *Hamlet* line, 'To be or not to be, that is the question', there is an extra unstressed beat at the end of the line, and a falling rhythm as the word 'question' trails off. Shakespeare is here using a 'feminine' ending to suggest irresolution. An example of a feminine rhyme would be: 'willow/billow'. Feminine rhymes are often used for comic effect, as in Humpty Dumpty or the Quangle Wangle. The more unstressed syllables there are to a rhyme, the more comic the effect.

masculine rhyme/ending
This is the politically incorrect term used to describe an effect the opposite of feminine rhyme/line ending. Masculine rhyme is the term used to describe a stressed rhyme (taste/waste); and 'masculine ending' of one or more stressed extra beats at the end of a line.

allusion
Either an echo or a quotation from another work, not usually signalled by quotation marks. Often referred to synonymously with 'intertextuality',

which is a broader term meaning the interconnections between texts.

foot

The term used for the unit of syllables by which we measure a poem's metrical pattern. A foot most commonly contains two syllables (as in iambic, trochaic, and spondaic metre). But there are further variations, such as dactyllic and anapaestic. A foot which misses a beat is called 'catalectic'; and a foot which introduces an extra beat is called 'hypercatalectic'.

iamb

An iamb is a two-syllable 'foot' in which the stress falls on the second syllable.

iambic pentameter

This is the most widely used line in English poetry. It has ten syllables, with five stresses or emphases, which fall on the second, fourth, sixth, eighth, and final syllables. Example from Gray's *Elegy*: 'The plowman homeward plods his weary way'. The effect is to produce a rising and falling rhythm, very close to the pattern of ordinary English speech.

Trochee

A trochee is the reverse of an iamb: the stress falls on the first syllable of a two-syllabled foot.

Trochaic metre

A passage of poetry which more or less consistently follows a trochaic pattern. The most famous example in English is Longfellow's *Hiawatha:*

> By the shore of Gitche Gumee,
> By the shining Big-Sea-Water,
> Stood the wigwam of Nokomis

Used on its own (as in consistent trochaic pentameter or tetrameter), trochaic metre it is less common than iambic; but it is very frequently used in combination with iambic. This introduces variety, usually for the sake of emphasis. Example from the famous *Hamlet* line again: 'To be or not to be, that is the question'. Here, the first six syllables are iambic; then in the seventh Shakespeare switches to trochaic. This emphasises the pause, followed by emphasis on 'that'.

spondee A spondee is a foot of two syllables, with the emphasis equally placed on both syllables. Usually introduced into iambic pentameter, for variety.

spondaic metre
A passage of poetry which more or less consistently follows a spondaic pattern.

dactyl
A foot of three syllables, with the emphasis falling on the first syllable. Whole lines or poems in this metre have a ponderous sound which is sometimes used for comic effect.

dactylic metre
A passage of poetry which more or less consistently follows a dactylic pattern.

anapaest
A foot of three syllables, the two first being unstressed and the last stressed.

anapaestic metre
A passage of poetry which more or less consistently follows an anapaestic pattern. Example of a line of anapaests: 'The Assyrian came down like the wolf on the fold' (Byron, *Destruction of Sennacharib*).

tetrameter
A tetrameter has eight syllables and four feet, usually iambic. An example of iambic tetrameter: 'Come live with me and be my love' (Marvell).

STAGE ONE

Trigger words, and the group's responses, for a sonnet of any type about the sea.

LAND'S END

1. DANIEL: suicide, freedom, conclusion
2. ALICE: break, descend, chartered
3. CAROLINE: foam, galloping, crash, drop, furthest, seamen
4. LIZZIE: salt, rough, history
5. BRENDAN: starfish, skunk
6. BEN: edge, furthermost, conclusion
7. LUCY: unfathomed, sheer, stray

SHELL

1. voices, loneliness, ghosts
2. echoes, worn, voiced
3. ribbed, curved, silky
4. raw, hollow, brittle, fragile
5. shock, ridges, unexploded
6. ear, stolen, borrower, pocket
7. tube, unheard, opal, pearly-twirly

NET

1. hooks, cutting
2. sized, unreasoned, constricting
3. orange, sieving, cut loose
4. thrashing, gasping, iridescent
5. profit, gills, trawls
6. entwined, wraith, waiting
7. snatch, hoard, dredge, found

SWELL

1. tempest, tantrum, flood
2. churn, loom, powerless
3. sails of ships, pregnant
4. curving, foam-topped, horses
5. five-and-dime, turgid, hankering, stand-by-me
6. rouse, rise, ruse, spume
7. spray, scatter, heave, envelope

DIVE

1. cleanse, baptism, weight
2. drown, drift
3. dart, dusk, land
4. breath, plunge, deep, smooth, sleek
5. seedy, wreck, underground, swing
6. plummet, sheer, penetrate, impulse
7. suffocate, no breath, vision

Group Poem on the Sea

LAND'S END

suicide freedom conclusion break descend
chartered foam galloping crash furthest seamen
salt rough history starfish skunk edge furthermost
conclusion unfathomed sheer stray

SHELL

voices loneliness ghosts echoes worn voiced
ribbed curved silky raw hollow brittle fragile
shock ridges unexploded ear stolen borrower
pocket tube unheard opal pearly-twirly

NET

hooks cutting sized unreasoned constricting
orange seiving cut loose thrashing gasping
iridescence profit gills trawls entwined
wraith waiting snatch hoard dredge found

SWELL

tempest tantrum flood churn loom powerless
sails of a ship pregnant foam-topped horses
curving five and dime turgid hankering stand-by-me
rouse rise ruse spume spray scatter heave envelope

DIVE

cleanse baptism weight drown drift dart duck land
breath plunge deep smooth sleek plummet sheer
penetrate impulse seedy wreck underground swing
suffocate no-breath vision

(lineation by Jenny Lewis)

Jenny Lewis

SHELL

It has the rough salt history of the sea
in it, the loneliness of ghosts worn thin
by echoes of belonging, talking in
siren sighs – *come join us, stand by me.*
To plummet down into that sheer, no-breath,
no-way-out tempest tantrum of flying spume,
to feel the galloping crash of the foam
curved and silky above you is no death
but freedom, conclusion, furthermost edge,
beyond the reach of every seaman's stare,
unhoarded, spare, unheard, uncharted,
a bare, ribbed-opal, starfish covered ridge,
as pearly and deep as an inner ear,
of brittle endings and things just started.

-- Jenny Lewis

Jenny Lewis introduces 'Shell'

I wrote out some of my personal favourites of the 'favourite' lines and was very taken with 'rough, salt, history'. It reminded me of Heaney's poetry which - like Tom Paulin's - is always informed by history. I liked the idea of a shell because it represented sea sounds which could take you deeply into the metaphor of the sea as consciousness and beyond consciousness (death?), but at the same time, the 'twirly whirly' association reminded me of the physical structure of an inner ear. So as an image it is simultaneously timeless, weightless, shapeless and a delicate physical reality. It is like using the physical to reach the metaphysical. Also, the 'inner ear' is like the 'inward eye', a site of intuition and ultra sensitivity, of memory and fantasy or 'Fancy' perhaps. I liked very much the 'galloping crash of the foam' for its forward acceleration, and the 'seaman's stare' came in useful with its resonances of *The Ancient Mariner* and *The Tempest.*

Lucy Newlyn writes a critical analysis

Jenny Lewis considers her 'shell' as a portion of the eternal. In its fragility, brittleness and smallness the shell is finite, and yet it also contains the timeless, the oceanic. We are alerted to the poem's preoccupation with the doubleness of temporality right from its arresting first line: 'It has the rough salt history of the sea/in it'. Here, Jenny plays with the paradoxical possibility of the vast being collapsed into the minuscule, or the eternal being apprehended through and in the temporal. The friction between an abstract noun, 'history', and two sensory adjectives, 'rough' and salt', brings into focus a possible tension between material and immaterial models of time. (The sea is a tangible entity we can taste and touch; while 'history' is elusive.) Enjambement reinforces this tension: the carefully run-on prepositional clause 'in it' at line 2 works almost as a containment of the vast un-ending sea in the preceding line. Conceptually, too, the poem plays with the paradoxical convergence of limits and limitlessness: at lines 9-10, the words 'conclusion' and 'furthest edge' are unexpectedly associated with freedom, lack of constraint.

While we are reading this poem, we are probably thinking of the sound made by a shell held to the ear – a sound as mysterious and unfathomable as the sea. As the poem develops, the shell comes metaphorically to be associated with language itself – with the connotative power of words as symbols. This association is confirmed by a simile in the penultimate line, likening the shell to an inner ear. The shell and the ear are both vessels of something profound and communicative, though not always within comprehension.

A sonnet is compact and intricately constructed, like a shell; but it can be the vehicle for vast and complex ideas. Many sonnet-writers have chosen this form to explore huge themes such as human mortality, spiritual devotion, or love. In such cases, the tightness of the form contrasts tellingly with the vastness of the subject-matter. Sonnets give writers the maximum potential for using connotative language concisely. Jenny makes the most of this potential in her handling of the form. Her sonnet draws attention to the symbolic potential of poetic language, its power to evoke big ideas. But it also creates the effect of ideas spilling out of their containment. A number of surprising features in the rhyme-scheme reinforce the sense, as we read or listen to the poem, that the form is being ruptured.

'Shell' is written in fairly regular iambic pentameter; but the rhyme-scheme is neither Petrarchan nor Shakespearean. The octave begins (as in Petrarchan) ABBA, but it then shifts to CDDC, with a full stop at the end of line 4, as if to emphasise that an expected unit is being broken. The sestet is also divided half way through: EFG EFG, creating an echoic effect appropriate to the aural simile of the shell as an ear. There is, too, an unexpected continuity between the second quatrain and the sestet, which comes from the use of enjambement. Lines 5-14 contain a single, long drawn out sentence with three main clauses (1: 'to plummet...spume'; 2: 'to feel...no death'; 3: but freedom...just started'), each of which is subdivided. The sentence's length causes the reader to hold his or her breath when reading the poem aloud, much as when reading Milton's long, rolling, syntactically convoluted passages of blank verse. Even if reading in one's head, the effect is much the same, for the eye follows the sense with some difficulty through each sub-clause to the conclusion. The moment at line 5 where 'no-breath' appears is the very moment at which the eye takes in the huge sentence that lies ahead. The syntax thus reinforces the sense one has of plunging headlong into a deep and breath-taking medium.

The poem's fluidity and energy come partly from the freedom with which Jenny has interpreted the sonnet's rules. But much also depends on her use of compound nouns as adjectives, and the multiplication of adjectival clauses – 'no-breath/ no-way-out tempest tantrum' 'bare, ribbed-opal, starfish covered'. Their repeated use creates an almost Hopkinsian diction, richly loaded with associative meaning. The preponderance of dactylic words – 'history', 'loneliness', 'galloping', 'furthermost' – contributes to the sense of ideas tumbling over each other, perhaps suggesting or miming the heady movement of waves. Most important of all, enjambement creates a charged and energetic momentum. Its sustained use throughout the sonnet concentrates the reader's mind (visually, rhythmically) on the relationship between endings and beginnings.

The closing line leaves us with a wittily epigrammatic summary of the poem's twin themes ('brittle endings and things just started') here joined together by the deliberately weak copula, 'and'. As well as being paradoxical, there is something almost bathetic about the phrase 'things just started' coming right at the end of the sonnet, where one might expect a climactic closure. Also, there is a sudden shift from high-register Miltonic syntax and lexicon (abstract nouns, as well as participial adjectives with negative prefixes such as 'unhoarded, unheard, uncharted') into the lower-register plainness of 'things', and 'started'. The overall effect of the last line is hard to describe. It is effortless and understated, almost throwaway: an effect heightened by the daring use of a weak (feminine) rhyme right at the end: 'uncharted'/'just started'. This bathetic tone reinforces the poem's meaning. The juxtaposition of grandiloquent with homely diction, and the use of an almost lame-sounding tail-piece together create the 'sublime' effect of truncation. The poem trails off into what Wordsworth called the 'something evermore about to be'.

Elizabeth Scott-Baumann edits

SHELL

Plummet down into that sheer, no-breath,
no-way-out tempest tantrum of flying spume,
feel the galloping crash of the foam
curved and silky.

Above you is no death
but freedom, conclusion, furthermost edge.

A bare, ribbed-opal, starfish covered ridge,
it has the rough salt history of the sea
and the loneliness of ghosts worn thin
by echoes of belonging,
as pearly and deep as an inner ear,
of brittle endings and things just started.

-- Elizabeth Scott-Baumann (after Jenny Lewis)

Lucy Newlyn edits

GHOSTS

Under a bare, ribbed-opal,
Starfish-covered ridge,

Ghosts talk in siren sighs:
"*Come join us, stand by me.*

Here is no death, but freedom;
Come join us, stand by me.

No death, but uttermost conclusion;
Come join us. Stand by me.

Plummet down into this flying spume;
Come join us, stand by me.

Feel the galloping crash of the foam;
Come join us, stand by me."

Under this bare, ribbed-opal,
Starfish-covered ridge,

Ghosts sing in siren sighs
The rough salt history of the sea.

-- Lucy Newlyn (after Jenny Lewis).

Note: Sirens have always fascinated me, so I developed Jenny's metaphorical handling of the siren theme into a whole poem. I found the line 'Come join us, stand by me' very haunting, and used it as a refrain. The sirens remain metaphorical, as in Jenny's poem, for they are the ghosts of those lost at sea. The new poem is about the temptation of oblivion, and the power of the dead over the living.

Lucy Newlyn

LAND'S END

No choughs, no curlews. Fathomless and free,
Beyond the furthest edge of now and here,
Where chartered land drops sudden, sheer
To rough salt history, the mystery
Begins of un-beginning sea.
Surging nearer, louder and more clear
Through blank unmeasured waste of then and there,
Sea-swell heaves, smashes, shatters on the scree.
Crusted rock-pools pocket the spume's leavings:
Stones worn silky-thin, an ammonite's rare coil,
Net, yarn, driftwood, a cork bobbing-bobbing,
Pearly-twirly shell-tubes, feathers tipped with oil.
Sculpted and re-sculpted by the tide's harsh grain
These souvenirs will vanish. Rock and sea remain.

-- Lucy Newlyn

Lucy Newlyn introduces 'Land's End'

This was my first ever sonnet, and I found it really difficult to write. The hardest bit was getting all the rhymes in the right order. First I trawled through all the words selected by the class, and chose the ones with the greatest resonance for me. Then I drafted the poem in iambic metre. Next I put in the rhymes, trying to keep to iambic pentameter. For a while the poem had longer and longer lines as it progressed, which made it look as well as sound like a wave:

> Ancient, fathomless and free,
> Beyond the furthest edge of now and here
> Where chartered land drops sudden, sheer
> To rough salt history, the sea
> Begins, the sea begins the mystery
> Of un-beginning sea. Advancing nearer and more clear
> Through empty unmeasured wastes of then and there,
> Sea-surge swells, urges, scatters, sways, sprays spume against the scree.
> In rock-pools, crevices, land pockets the sea's leavings:
> Stones worn silky thin, an ammonite's rare coil,
> Net, yarn, driftwood, a cork bobbing-bobbing,
> Pearly lobes and twirly-whirly tubes of shells, gulls' feathers tipped with oil.
> Swallowed and spewed, swallowed and spewed,
> The sea preserves in old economy what land steals back from memory.

I was quite attracted to the idea of leaving it like that; but I wanted to discipline myself, so I edited the whole thing through, sticking to iambic pentameter throughout, with some minor variants.

As far as the rhyme scheme goes, the sonnet is a mongrel. I took a Petrarchan style octave and grafted onto it a Shakespearean sestet, concluding with a couplet. I wanted a strong volta at the octave, as the poem turns from the vastness of the sea to what it throws up on the land. I wanted the octave to be sublime and the sestet to be intricate, detailed – like an inventory. In the couplet I wanted to resolve the dichotomy of sea and land. Originally my final couplet broke away too much from the rest of the poem. I wanted more of a sense that the sea and land were working in collaboration. I also wanted the poem to end with a suggestion of the permanence of nature contrasted with the impermanence of memories and artefacts – 'souvenirs'.

I think the inventory works. I am not so sure about the sublimity of the octave: it sounds like a cross between Wordsworth and Shelley on a bad day. It is hard for me to tackle the sea's sublimity without being Romantic about it: the whole exercise made me realise that a poem has to be oblique and angled to be effective.

Jenny Lewis writes a critical analysis

In 'Land's End' Lucy uses the octave to paint the coastal and marine landscape with broad brushstrokes. By listing what is *not* there, we get a sense of emptiness, boundless space and of being taken beyond known limits. This is underlined by the inversion of the phrase 'here and now' to 'now and here'. 'Surging nearer, louder,' captures the approaching sound of the sea from far-off. The accelerating onomatopaiea of 'louder', 'smashes', 'shatters' is particularly effective in bringing the reader to the brink of the more intimate experience which has been set up in the sestet.

The *volta* of the sestet switches the focus of the reader from wide open spaces to a miniaturist close-up of fine details. This inventory of delicate things includes stones 'worn silky-thin', 'an ammonite's rare coil', 'Net, yarn, driftwood, a cork bobbing-bobbing' as well as 'Pearly-twirly shell-tubes' and 'feathers tipped with oil'. This beachcomber's trove is described in line 14 as 'souvenirs' – a catalogue of small things to be taken away and hoarded in a way that the larger elements of rock, sea and tides cannot. These can only be internalised and kept in the memory for as long as the individual lives. In just such a way, the words themselves become like a collector's hoard, each bearing its own reservoir of associations and memories.

The sonnet has a Petrarchan octave – ABBA, ABBA, and a Shakespearean sestet – CDCD, EE. The feeling of closure given by the final couplet emphasises the poem's theme which is the contrast between the ephemeral and the eternal. The first two lines, in iambic pentameter, shelve down into tetrameter in the third line, suggesting the suddenness of a cliff dropping away. Line four can be stressed either as tetrameter or pentameter and the fifth line becomes pentameter again, suggesting the ebbing and flowing of the sea. The trochaic pentameter of line six conjures the sense of a tidal force surging through into the more measured iambic pentameter of the following line – 'Through blank unmeasured waste of then and there'.

Although Milton avoided couplets as being too reductive, the couplet at the end of 'Land's End' works marvellously well to encapsulate the theme of the ephemeral set against the eternal. The words 'Land's End' themselves carry the resonance of the Celtic legends and a buried sub-text of magic, shape-changing and other-worldliness. The choughs (soul-carriers) have already gone on ahead carrying the souls of our ancestors. Now it's as if the land we stand on is transforming itself into unfixed elements of sea and air and we are invited to cast away our material form and merge with them; but instead we stand at the edge with the small tokens which evidence our humanity – shells, nets, driftwood, corks – awed by and fearful of what is to come.

Elizabeth Scott-Baumann edits

LAND'S END

No choughs, no curlews. Fathomless and free,
Beyond the furthest edge of now and here,

Stones worn silky-thin,
an ammonite's rare coil,

Where chartered land drops sudden, sheer
To rough salt history,

Net, yarn, driftwood,
a cork bobbing-bobbing,

The mystery begins of un-beginning sea.
Surging nearer, louder and more clear

Pearly-twirly shell-tubes
feathers tipped with oil.

Crusted rock-pools pocket the spume's leavings:
Sculpted and re-sculpted by the tide's harsh grain

These souvenirs will vanish.
Rock and sea remain.

-- Elizabeth Scott-Baumann (after Lucy Newlyn)

NOTE: I thought that the echoic tone of this sonnet could be emphasised by dividing it into smaller stanzas with an echoic refrain composed of the souvenirs themselves which pervaded the original sonnet. I think it has a softer, more wistful tone.

Jenny Lewis edits

LAND'S END

No choughs, no
curlews, fathomless:
beyond the furthest edge
chartered land
drops

sheer, un-beginning,
surging louder
through blank wastes

the sea-swell heaves
and smashes

rock-pools pocket
spume's leavings –

stones
silky thin

ammonite's
rare coil,

net
yarn
driftwood
a cork
                    bobbing-bobbing

pearly-twirly
shell tubes, feathers
tipped with oil

sculpted and re-sculpted,
these souvenirs will vanish:

rock and sea
remain.

-- Jenny Lewis after Lucy Newlyn

NOTE: I wanted to free the language from the strictures of the rhymed sonnet form. I also thought it was appropriate to experiment with shape and try using spaces more experimentally. I put the sestet into list form, with 'bobbing-bobbing' set in a playful position as if bobbing away from the main island of text into a sea of space.

Caroline Boon edits

LAND'S END

Beyond the furthest edge of now and here,
Where chartered land drops sudden, sheer,
No choughs, no curlews. Fathomless and free,
Sea-swell heaves, smashes, shatters on the scree.
Sculpted and re-sculpted by the tide's harsh grain
Crusted pools pocket, the spume's leavings remain.

Surging nearer, louder and more clear
Through blank unmeasured waste of then and there,
In rough salt history the mystery
Of un-beginning sea.

-- Caroline Boon (after Lucy Newlyn)

In editing Lucy's poem I really wanted to play around with her rhyme scheme. I was interested to see how much sense her poem would make with the lines rearranged. I thought 'no choughs, no curlews' was too abrupt as a beginning which is why I moved it to appear later in the poem. I loved the descriptions of the movement of the sea and I think the new rhyme scheme allows this to figure more powerfully in the poem now.

Elizabeth Scott-Baumann

TAKE ME THERE

Take me to the furthest land's end edge
Where the stony story of this isle waits,
While in the silent deep the rope wraiths dredge
For foil flicker fish thrashed by hook and weights.
Talk to me when the white shell at my ear
Speaks not pearly words but the hollow roar
Of silence. The unheard I should not hear,
The voiced unexploded shock of sea floor.
Hold me as the soda swell horses loom
As the surging flood fall crescendo lifts,
The foam topped tempest tantrum spews forth spume
Then calm. Sails straighten and the wave curve drifts.
Kiss me as I stand like a fragile shell
Like a deep sleek dive down with my breath held.

-- Elizabeth Scott-Baumann

Elizabeth Scott-Baumann introduces 'Take Me There'

I wrote this almost immediately after the class in which we collected response words to the trigger words (in this case: Land's end, shell, net, swell and dive). The element of the class which inspired me most was the aural juxtaposition and conjunction this process stimulated. This often leads to connections which would not usually occur in ordinary speech patterns. I found these unexpected clashes and echoes intriguing, and particularly resonant in evoking the reverberations of the sea's motion. Although each line is ten syllables, the dominance of unusual aural configurations diffuses the conventional iambic pentameter of sonnets. In the Shakespearean form the rhyme scheme (ABAB, CDCD, EFEF, GG) falls naturally into three quatrains and a couplet which I emphasised by drawing in elements of a blessing. I wanted the invocations ('take me', 'talk to me', 'hold me', 'kiss me') to resonate in an echoing and almost elegiac refrain while retaining the essence of the sonnet structure.

Ben Burton writes a critical analysis

'Take Me There' absorbs the reader. This process begins the moment the poem is taken up, as the reader is called upon to determine whether the words 'take me' are to be spoken as a command, a plea, or simply a request. As no other character but the speaker is mentioned in the sonnet, Lizzie allows one to infer that the line is directed at the reader who, through reading this sonnet, shall 'take' the speaker through their journey. This sense of accompaniment is suggested again when the speaker makes a second appeal:

> Talk to me when the white shell at my ear
> Speaks not pearly words but the hollow roar
> Of silence. [ll 5-7]

The absence of reassuring 'pearly words' is made all the more discomforting by the prevalence of pararhymes in these lines: *ear*, p*ear*ly, w*or*ds, r*oar*, as if to suggest that the 'ear' meets only with distorting echoes inside the hollow shell. This dissonance continues with the oxymoronic 'hollow roar/

Of silence'. However, as the reader reads these lines, particularly when out loud, not only is the speaker's discomfort expressed, but also the request 'talk to me' fulfilled. Paradoxically, it is through reading that one breathes life into the 'hollow roar' of 'silent' words upon the page – another 'white shell' – and so continues to 'take' the speaker on their journey through the poem. This interpretation may shed light upon the compelling ambiguity of 'the voiced unexploded shock of sea-floor'. The management of time in this line may describe the process of writing and reading which binds speaker and reader in the poem – the text is 'voiced' – already written, expressing another's thoughts, and yet it exists 'unexploded'; those thoughts do not exist until they are re-created – and re-written by the act of reading. The 'shock' of this experience signifies what Wolfgang Iser describes as the 'inherently dynamic character' of the literary work: 'The convergence of text and reader brings the literary work into existence, and this convergence can never be precisely pinpointed, but must always remain virtual, as it is not to be identified either with the reality of the text or with the individual disposition of the reader.'

It is significant in this light that Lizzie should choose to reprise the image of the shell in the closing lines of the sonnet: 'Kiss me as I stand like a fragile shell', for the reader has indeed given the 'kiss' of life to the 'fragile shell' of this text, and has simultaneously taken the speaker, and been taken by them, through each line. The final line perhaps best captures this dynamic interaction – 'like a deep sleek dive down with my breath held' – in which the words 'dive down' oscillate between verb and adverb on the one hand, and noun and adjective on the other. Lizzie's sparse, impressionistic syntax preserves the ambiguity, leaving the reader to re-write the line each time they return to it; embarking upon a journey that is never the same twice.

Caroline Boon edits

TAKE ME THERE

Talk to me when the white shell at my ear speaks not pearly words but the hollow roar of silence. Take me to the furthest land's end edge where the stony story of this isle waits, while in the silent deep the rope wraiths dredge for foil flicker fish thrashed by hook and weights. Hold me as the soda swell horses loom as the surging flood fall crescendo lifts the foam topped tempest tantrum spews forth spume.

Like a deep sleek dive down with my breath held, kiss me as I stand like a fragile shell.

-- Caroline Boon (after Elizabeth Scott-Baumann)

NOTE: Lizzie's poem is full of adjectives which creates a sense of urgency. I compressed the lines to increase the intensity.

Ben Burton edits

TAKE ME THERE

Take me to the furthest land's end edge
Where the stony story of this isle waits,
Where the rope wraiths dredge
For flicker fish thrashed by hook and weights.
Talk to me when the white shell at my ear
Speaks not pearly words but the unheard,
Unexploded shock of sea floor.
Hold me as the surging flood fall crescendo lifts,
The foam topped tempest tantrum spews forth spume
Then calm. Sails straighten and the wave curve drifts.
Kiss me as I stand like a fragile breeze
Like a deep sleek dive down with my breath held.

--Ben Burton after Elizabeth Scott-Baumann.

I have attempted to produce a more sinewy version of the sonnet, bringing out its verbal strength by stripping away some adjectives. The body of the sonnet remains largely intact except for the excision of line 9: 'the soda swell horses loom.' I think this drop in register seems out of place in such an imposing section. The second quatrain has also been abbreviated in an attempt to increase the sense of mystery that surrounds the 'unexploded shock of sea floor.' I offer the image 'fragile breeze' in line 12 of this edit. Whilst this is hugely inferior to the original line, I wanted to ask whether using 'shell' twice in so short a poem might not detract from the haunting image in line 5.

Ben Burton

A SOFT REVOLT

Soft, what is that silent roar? Sea stolen
Away for us to share though far from shore.
There, do you hear the mere circulation;
Where innocent dreams immersed us before,
Moonstruck, to my ear immerse us once more.
Ours now then, this curving salty call
That swims within when I stop to hear.
Or is it only the shadow of my soul
Upthrown, my blood-song that holds me in thrall?
Say you hear it too, what then? Say we heard
Each for ourself alone, clutching this shell
In now unsure and nocent depths, where words
Make way like air from a drowning embrace
Soft, what is that, this sheer roaring silence?

-- Ben Burton

Ben Burton introduces 'A Soft Revolt'

I arrived upon the idea for this sonnet very quickly, taking as my starting point a passage from James Joyce's 'Ulysses'. In this passage the 'hero', Harold Bloom, observes that what people really hear when they hold a shell to their ear is '[their] blood.... Souse in the ear sometimes.' I wanted to see whether a love-sonnet, based around the sounds heard in a shell, could survive this revelation. I was surprised by the range of interpretations my poem drew from members of the class. I have always supported the theory that an author's intention can never be fully known from a text, but felt rather squeamish when I discovered how this theory affected the reception of my own poem. Could other readers share in the meaning I had spent so long developing in my poem, or was it inevitable that each would discover their own interpretation? I think I will be spending a little while longer mourning the 'death of the author.'

Elizabeth Scott-Baumann writes a critical analysis

Ben Burton's 'A Soft Revolt' is a Sidneyan sonnet (ABAB, BCBC, CDCD, EE) and the adoption of this form indicates an embrace of the theme of love. The allusion in the title to Shelley's *The Revolt of Islam* evokes powerful images of struggle and renewal, and a profound connection between love and conflict. The majority of lines start with a monosyllable increasing the impetus forward created by the trochaic pentameter. When lines start with a polysyllabic word its active gesture is emphasised by the trochaic rhythm, 'Away', 'Moonstruck', 'Upthrown'. While the trochaic pentameter charges this poem with energetic movement, the prevalence of pararhymes such as more/hear, call/soul, shell/thrall, diffuses the energy from strident sing-song to contemplative incantation. (See glossary for the use of pararhyme).

The first line is loaded with incantatory power as the 'soft' can be read both as an appeal to the reader or imagined listener, and in reference to the roar. The latter resonance is emphasised by the internal echo of 'soft' and 'silent'. The sussuration continues with 'Sea stolen' and is then abruptly broken off with 'Away'. The lulling alliteration is stolen away, as the poet perceives the sea to be. Similarly, by virtue of its position, 'Moonstruck' strikes the reader and forces him/her to pause in the same way as the poet. The reader is struck into pausing by the rhythm of the poem, as the poet is awe-struck by the resonating sound of the shell. Both pause to contemplate.

The connection between the lovers and the sea is established by the awe-inspiring complicity in stealing away the sea, and the aural and structural parallelism of 'share' and 'shore'. The word 'circulation', foregrounded by its Latinate diction and startling prefix of 'mere', evokes the movement of blood, in itself both the 'shadow of my soul' (life force) and the blood in one's ear which produces the 'blood-song', the movement of air and sound within the shell, the circularity of the shell, the ear, the body, the shore, and the eternal circulation of wave and tide. The shell calls up the 'shadow of my soul' in that the action of blood is the shadow of the soul as the roar of the shell is the shadow of the roar of the sea. The shell also calls up the 'shadow of my soul' in that the experience resonates in the relationship between the 'us' of the poem. Both the love and the beloved could be seen metaphysically as the 'shadow of my soul'. The phrase 'Ours now then' employs the same technique of offering both colloquial and literal meanings as the initial 'Soft'. 'Then' can be read as a colloquial qualification to the main sense, 'Ours now', but it can also function to express the fusion of time within the relationship of the two figures. 'Ours now then' can be read as a commitment to the 'us' in the present and in the past, and, implicit in the sea symbol of change which is timeless and constant, inevitably in the future. This pattern continues in the lines,

> Say you hear it too, what then? Say we heard
> Each for ourself alone, clutching this shell

Here 'say' can function either as 'tell' or as 'imagine if'. Both potential meanings imply doubt and the need for reassurance, and the following lines can be seen to provide that reassurance. The poet separates himself from the other as he is certain only in his experience. However, in the phrase 'Each for ourself alone' this distinction is combined with unity. Each individual hears the roar for him/herself, and this certainty of individual experience makes its shared quality more sound. The poet and the other hear it for themselves, not because of each other, and in both hearing it independently they are brought together, both clutching the shell.

The transferred epithet 'curving' generates meaning in the ambiguity of its referent. The 'call' of shell and blood cannot literally be seen as curving so the reader's imagination is drawn upon to refer 'curving' to the shoreline, the body of the beloved or the intricate structure of shell or ear. The resonance of 'thrall' is intensified by the characteristically Anglo-Saxon compound 'blood-song', and the framing allusion to *The Revolt of Islam.* The return of the poem to a variation on the first line embodies the circularity and curve explored by the poem. While 'drowning embrace' is a painful image of the interconnection of love and death, the chiming of 'silence' with 'embrace' suffuses the sense of circularity with a sense of resolution and hope.

Elizabeth Scott-Baumann edits

A SOFT REVOLT

Soft,
What is that silent roar? Sea stolen
Away for us to share though far from shore.

There,
do you hear the mere circulation;
Where innocent dreams immersed us before.

Moonstruck,
To my ear immerse us once more.
Ours now then, this curving salty call

Call,
That swims within when I stop to hear.
Or is it only the shadow of my soul

Upthrown,
my blood-song that holds me in thrall?
Say you hear it too, what then?

Say,
We heard each for ourself alone, clutching this shell
In now unsure and nocent depths.

Soft,
what is that, this sheer roaring silence?

-- Elizabeth Scott-Baumann (after Ben Burton)

Note: I wanted to emphasise the dislocation and need for affirmation in this sonnet, by dislocating the verses and placing an ambiguous, echoing, questioning word at the start of each verse. I think this creates a breathlessness, a questioning tone and embodies the need for affirmation before continuation. I was mostly able to divide up the existing poem but added 'call' to the fourth stanza which echoes the previous stanza. The word 'call' works as a command, a request and a description of a perceived feature, the salty call of stanza three. The absence of the final line enacts the silence spoken of in the poem.

Caroline Boon edits

A SOFT REVOLT

Soft, what is that silent roar?
Sea stolen away for us to share
Though far from shore.

There, do you hear the mere circulation;
Where innocent dreams immersed us before,
Moonstruck, to my ear immerse us once more.

Ours now this curving salty call
That swims within when I stop to hear.
Or is it only the shadow of my soul upthrown,
My blood-song that holds me in thrall?

Say you hear it too, what then?
Say we heard each for ourself alone,
In now unsure and nocent depths, where words
Make way like air from a drowning embrace…

Soft, what is that, this sheer roaring silence?

-- Caroline Boon (after Ben Burton)

NOTE: Not a lot has been edited here. I felt the need to spread Ben's lines out to create pauses within the poem and to emphasize the 'hush' created by the final line.

Lucy Newlyn edits

SEA STOLEN AWAY

Ours now then, this curving
salty call that swims within
when I stoop to hear.

Or is it only my soul upthrown,
my own bloodsong
holds me in thrall?

Say you hear it too,
what then?
what is that silent roar?

-- Lucy Newlyn (after Ben Burton)

Note: I wanted to pare the original down to the minimum, and to get rid of the allusions and archaic language, which I thought cluttered the poem. I loved the idea that picking up a shell was like stealing the sea, so the first thing I did in editing was to invent a new title using Ben's metaphor. I was aware that in doing so I was making the poem more my own: 'stealing it away', so to speak. I used triplets for compression and simplicity. Ending with the question was intended to create an eerie and enigmatic feeling.

Charlene Dy

EATING THE OCEAN

We scooped their bony selves with slender nets
From sea to baskets woven from supple sticks,
To be jostled till black and broken spines fell slick
Upon the sand, their bodies now stripped and wet.

When cradled in our palms, the stern touch
Of two insistent thumbs could crack their hulls,
Revealing orange tongues lying curled
As if asleep inside their fragile skulls.

We ate them then, acutely self-aware
Of tasting tongue on tongue, intensely thrilled
At the thought of eating creatures freshly killed.
But how did they taste, that barbarous ocean fare?

Raw, dissolving, sea-salted and sweet –
With carcasses of urchins scattered at our feet.

-- Charlene Dy

Charlene Dy introduces 'Eating the Ocean'

My sonnet was composed separately from the workshop process, as I had been unable to attend the first session. It does not therefore draw on the communal word-pool for ideas or imagery. I joined the workshop for subsequent sessions.

The sonnet, somewhat unusually I suppose, is a narrative rather than a lyric poem. While I composed it, one of Heaney's sonnets lurked in the back of my mind. It too was narrative in style, and was about acquiring a sunlight in his home. Heaney obviously being a more masterful poet than I, managed to take a simple story and through skilled used of metaphor, turn it into myth. His poem used the *volta* very stylishly, and alluded both to his relationship with his wife and the Biblical story of Jesus' healing of the paralysed. My poem, regrettably, stays firmly descriptive, and doesn't richly imbue the narrative account with significance. In a sense, it is just a streamlined, intensified memory. Our family has a favourite beach, and the first time we went, we realised we couldn't safely play in the water due to an over-proliferation of sea-urchins, which if stepped on, are both painful and poisonous. The problem was creatively solved when an old fisherman came down and showed us how to eat them, raw. Sea urchin roe, also called uni, is a Japanese delicacy, and it was odd for us to be taking that food out of its refined and artful context – we ate it like savages really, on the beach. But all that was very difficult to condense into a sonnet, so instead of relinquishing richness of detail and accuracy of description (because I thought the image of the sea-urchins was visually arresting), I sacrificed 'plot'. I was hoping the effect would be a little like Elizabeth Bishop's 'Crusoe in England', where you have beautiful imagery of an environment with which an aggravated, ambiguous character interacts.

Two notes on technical difficulties: 1, tense can be inconsistent, since the account is narrative, and thus temporally defined. 2, the *volta* comes before the last couplet, near the end, rather than in the middle.

Brendan Jones writes a critical analysis

Charlene's poem consists of three quatrains, each with an independent rhyme scheme, and closes with a rhymed couplet. The 14 lines are generally five-foot iambics, and the quatrains use the petrarchan rhyme scheme of ABBA but it has a Shakespearan couplet to end it.

Formally, the poem juxtaposes hard with soft, contrasting 'bony selves' with 'supple sticks,' 'stern touch' with 'fragile skull', 'cracked' hulls and 'orange tongues'. The hard 'k' sound, introduced in the opening line with the word 'scooped' is repeated throughout the poem in words such as 'baskets' and 'broken', 'crack' and 'skulls'. This abrasive sound is balanced by the repetition of soothing, even soporific 's' sounds in words like 'slender' and 'slick' and 'asleep'. Occasionally Charlene combines the two soft and hard sounds in words such as 'scooped' and 'baskets' and 'skulls'.

Like the Petrarchan sonnet, the poem introduces a problem by juxtaposing brute force driven by hunger with the sea urchins stolen from the sea, then asks whether or not it is 'barbarous' to use such a 'stern touch' against the 'fragile' urchins, as they are without defence, even described as 'asleep'. After stating the problem in the first three quatrains, Charlene writes: 'But how did they taste, that barbarous ocean fare?' The emotional tension of whether a food, so cruelly won, can be eaten in good faith, and actually taste good, sets up the couplet. Echoing William Carlos Williams' description of plums from the freezer, Charlene describes the creatures as 'Raw, dissolving, sea-salted and sweet –'. The first term seems self-evident, the second is almost a scientific observation, the third and rational sensual reaction (they came from the sea, thus it must have been the sea which salted them) and the fourth a pleasurable sensual reaction, as most people enjoy sweet foods. The closing line of the poem reads 'With carcasses of urchins scattered at our feet.' Of the hard/soft juxtaposition, the 'soft' has been processed by the senses and body, resulting in the word 'sweet', while the hard shells (deceptively described as 'carcasses') exist as reminders of the 'barbarous' nature of the eating. The poem functions similarly on a phonetic level: the first line of the couplet is dominated by the soft 's': 'dissolving', 'sea-salted', 'sweet' while in the closing line the 'K' sound takes over: 'carcasses', 'urchins', 'scattered'. All that remains are the hard shells.

The poem is remarkable when describing the specific actions involved in eating urchins: the 'scooping' and 'stern touch' needed to 'crack their hulls'. Similarly, the comparison of the 'We' (the eaters) with 'orange tongues lying curled/as if asleep in their fragile skulls' works very well. The two are united in a remarkable sensual image of 'tongue on tongue.'

Structurally, I think the poem could be tightened if certain words, usually occupying the space of the 8th and 9th syllable, were taken out. For example, in the second line 'supple' could be removed, while in the 7th line 'lying' could be removed, and in the 10th line, 'intensely' could be removed. Also I believe that the attentive reader, upon reading the marvellous closing couplet, would implicitly understand the question being asked by observing the answer expressed in the couplet. Thus the 12th line, which also seems to freeze the sensual rhythm of the sonnet, could be taken out.

In the end, the careful working of sounds and images in 'Eating the Ocean' come together to create a stunning sensuality that causes one to question not only the ingestion of urchins, but also the very act of eating in the first place.

Ben Burton edits

EATING THE OCEAN

We scooped their bony selves
with slender nets
from sea to baskets
woven from supple sticks
and upon the sand
broken spines fell slick
their bodies stripped and wet
when cradled in our palms

the stern touch
of two insistent thumbs
could crack their hulls
revealing orange tongues
inside their fragile skulls
lying curled as if asleep.

We ate them acutely
aware of tongue on tongue
intensely thrilled
at the thought of creatures
freshly killed.
But how did they taste,
that barbarous ocean fare?

Raw, dissolving,
sea-salted and sweet –
With carcases of urchins
scattered at our feet.

-- Ben Burton (after Charlene Dy)

Elizabeth Scott-Baumann edits

EATING THE OCEAN

We scooped their bony selves with slender nets from sea to baskets
Woven from supple sticks, to be
Jostled till black and broken spines
Fell slick upon the sand, their bodies now
Stripped and wet.
Cradled in our palms, the stern touch of two insistent thumbs could
Crack their hulls,
Revealing orange tongues lying
Curled as if asleep inside their fragile skulls.

We ate them then, acutely self-aware of tasting tongue on tongue,
intensely
Thrilled at the thought of
Eating creatures freshly
Killed. But how did they taste, that barbarous ocean fare?

Raw, dissolving, sea-salted and sweet –
With carcasses of urchins scattered at our feet.

-- Elizabeth Scott-Baumann (after Charlene Dy)

NOTE: This is very much just an experiment. I have made each line start with a verb, the two first main sections starting with a communal action, 'We scooped', 'we ate'. These first lines are long, difficult to get through, conveying the process of transition for 'we scooped' and the breathless excitement and absorption for 'we ate'. I think the focus on verbs emphasises the anxiety of the poet narrator with the actions carried out upon the sea urchins. I moved the reflective answer to the final question away from the main body of the poem to a sense of dialogue or even dichotomy between the poet's experience and her reflection on that experience.

Brendan Jones

you love like a skunk i mean a starfish

you love like a skunk i mean a starfish
five arms splayed stuck to my hull thousand lips
sucking the bulwarks you are afraid of
brittleness and spend hours in front of
the mirror clogged with brine and pearly-twirly
sea grit pouring salt in your pores
you love profit i've seen you in action
eyes bulged out like marbles tongue licking
my account as if it were a golden rib
you cling to the plank after the
barnacles have fallen dug into my flank
and always re-growing feasting while we sink
at three in the morning long after
the lifeboats have given up rowing

-- Brendan Jones

Brendan Jones introduces 'you love like a skunk i mean a starfish'

The poem attempts to capture the tone of a writer slipping into insanity as a result of another person whose presence has become suffocating. The first line shows the attempt of the poet trying to put a finger on the appropriate simile, and finally finding it – a starfish. 'Four arms' suggests a human being (four limbs), while 'thousand lips/sucking at my bulwarks' points to a superhuman effort to hang on, or cling, as well as to undo the foundations or 'bulwarks' of the thing – or person – being attacked. Being afraid of 'brittleness' suggests that that attacker has issues around age, as well as problems with self-appearance: 'hours in front of the mirror'. But the problems of appearance, 'clogged with sea-grit', are actually the result of 'clinging to the bulwarks' – that is, of being so attached to something that no time remains for self-maintenance.

In the first line of the octet the poem changes course into a meditation on why this person is so attached and suggests that it could be a love of money: 'you love profit'. This idea is tied up with sex as well as biblical origins of the female: 'licking/my account as if it were a rib'. The poem then moves back from meaning to description, once again suggesting a tenacity on the part of the person outlasting any sort of natural cycle: 'you cling to the plank long after the barnacles have fallen', and 'dug into my flank' as well as the gift, or curse in this case, of always 're-growing'. Finally, the poem ends with an image of this person/starfish finding sustenance, but at the same time killing that which it feeds on, as friends interested in helping out have long since given up.

> feasting while we sink
> at three in the morning long after
> the lifeboats have given up rowing

On a formal level, the first three lines of the poem each contain ten syllables with a caesura splitting each line into five syllables. The poem is slowed down with the opening dactyl of the fourth line in 'brittleness'. The speed of the line is halted once more in the fifth line with the amphibrach 'the mirror'. The opening of lines four and five function to slow down a poem moving pell-mell toward the tenth-floor window, calming the poet as well as the reader, as if to say 'relax', 'get hold of yourself'.

The fifth line, relaxed, lapses into iambic pentameter with an extra last syllable or hypercatalectic. The feet alternate between iambs, trochees and anapaests, and this continues until the eighth line, when the poem once again gathers speed, starting with molossus of 'eyes bulged out'. The metre alternates again until the eleventh line, when the poem takes on the anapaestic trimeter hypercatalectic which will also structure the 12th line.

In the final couplet, the poem switches to anapaestic trimeter catalectic with an iamb at the beginning of the line. In the final five lines a rhyming sequence, mostly internal, is introduced, focusing on 'ing' rhymes – regrowing, feasting, moving, rowing. The repeated anapaests give the lines a feel of the incantation, a soporific magic spell, perhaps suggesting a slip into semi-consciousness or even insanity on the poet's part.

Charlene Dy writes a critical analysis

I thought at first that this was a love poem, but have since changed my mind. It is a poem of resistance, endurance, and perhaps love, but what distinguishes it is its refusal to be pinned down. What first strikes the reader is the sonnet's aggressively non-traditional form. Pointedly disregarding capitalisation, punctuation, end-rhyme, elevated diction, and iambic pentameter, the only thing Brendan retains of the traditional sonnet form is the fourteen-line stanza. These rather obvious acts of defiance would seem almost juvenile, except that the rules are broken to such breathtaking effect that the reader quickly relents, agreeing to read the poem on the poet's own terms.

Formally, the lack of punctuation allows for certain phrases to take on multiple meanings, such as in the lines, 'sucking the bulwarks you are afraid of/ brittleness and spend hours in front of/ the mirror'. In the phrase 'you are afraid of', the object of fear could refer either to the 'bulwarks' or to 'brittleness', making us wonder about the motivations behind the starfish's metaphorical and insistent clinging. Is the creature attached to a boat that she is also afraid of, or is the attachment fuelled by a sense of self-loathing and insecurity? This allows for a complexity of emotion to develop, and for wide interpretation; the poem can act like a musical score without notation: each reading brings a new poem, a poem with a different cadence or a different voice.

Even as conventional uses of rhyme and metre are dispensed with, they are re-introduced in different, often subversive, but not always successful ways. In terms of metre and line-length, the poem runs the gamut, with lines anywhere between eight to twelve syllables long. While the flexibility lets the poet play with tone (slower and more sombre with irregular stresses, or quick and even, etc), he relinquishes his power to make statements with his lines. Disarmed of both punctuation and iambic pentameter, they seem weakened – barely lines at all – a matter not helped by the use of feminine line-endings and forgettable end words: 'of', 'after the'.

Brendan is metrically more successful in his repeated us of the spondee, especially at the beginning of lines. The unbroken stresses of 'you love', 'five arms', and 'sea-grit' give the poem a rhythmic intensity and sonic weight which complement the heavy-handed 'love' that characterises the poem's starfish. Similarly, Brendan's use of internal rhyme achieves a grounding effect. Almost always sneaked into unexpected places, the rhymes surprise, even as they unify the poem. The last lines, with their onslaught of re-growing / feasting / cling / morning / rowing give the poem a sense of closure and finality with their melancholic repetition.

In his images, too, Brendan never ceases to surprise and startle. With a bold pen, he mixes the sensual and the grotesque to illuminate a relationship where love is as parasitical as it is enduring. Over the course of the poem, he alternately describes the starfish as a creature with 'thousand lips/ sucking', and with 'eyes bulged out like marbles', rendering it both lover and beast. One moment, the starfish is 'licking' and in the next, the same action is described as 'feasting while we sink'. As readers, we are not allowed to grow complacent, not granted the ease of certainty. Each understanding we develop of the relationship is twisted in the next line. If we are starfish hoping to keep a firm hold on the poem, we will be thwarted, even as the boat has sunk by the poem's end. The relationship of boat and starfish serves not only as a conceit for two lovers, but for the relationship between the poem and the reader.

What interests me most, however, is that while the poem eschews almost all of the sonnet tradition, it nevertheless brings to mind one of the most beloved and canonised sonnets in English literature: Shakespeare's Sonnet 116. It, too, describes a love which persists, it too uses the metaphor of the lover/beloved as a boat or 'bark', and it too ends the poem with an image of a love carrying on until 'the edge of doom'. The genius of Brendan's poem perhaps lies in the fact that he continues what the Bard merely suggested. Brendan's boat sinks, not only venturing to the edge of doom, but drowning in it – with the starfish still holding on, albeit discarding the sonnet tradition on its way down.

Caroline Boon edits

you love like a skunk i mean a starfish

you love like a skunk i mean a starfish
five arms splayed
stuck to my hull thousand lips
sucking the bulwarks

you are afraid of brittleness
and spend hours in front of the mirror
clogged with brine and pearly-twirly
sea grit pouring salt in your pores

you love profit i've seen you in action
eyes bulged out like marbles tongue licking
my account as if it were a golden rib
you cling to the plank after the barnacles have fallen

dug into my flank, always re-growing
feasting while we sink
at three in the morning long after
the lifeboats have given up rowing

-- Caroline Boon (after Brendan Jones)

NOTE: I haven't changed much about this poem. It was perhaps the hardest to edit, and my editing involved mostly playing with the line endings to see how the sense of the poem was affected.

Lucy Newlyn edits

STARFISH

You love like a skunk – I mean a starfish:
five arms splayed, stuck to my hull,
a thousand lips sucking the bulwarks.

You are afraid of brittleness
and spend hours in front of the mirror,
clogged with brine and pearly-twirly sea-grit

pouring salt into your pores.
You love profit:
I've seen you in action,

eyes bulged out like marbles,
tongue licking my account
as if it were a golden rib.

You cling to the plank
after the barnacles have fallen,
dug into my flank and always re-growing,

feasting while we sink at three
in the morning, long after the lifeboats
have given up rowing.

-- Lucy Newlyn (after Brendan Jones)

Note: I wanted to uncover the most straightforward way of reading the syntax of this poem, by supplying its ‘missing’ punctuation. The language reminds me of some of Sylvia Plath’s writing, so I tried using a favourite form of hers, the triplet (a three line, unrhymed stanza). I did not want to change anything else in this very subtle and powerful poem.

Caroline Boon

IN CONSTANCY

Silky morning starfish light
Through yonder window breaks
Rushing sounds of foamy white
Waves greet me as I wake
The pearly rays of pregnant dawn
Give birth to a heaving crescendo
Mounted by fishing boats trawling the morn
Guarding their hoard in the hastening glow.
And salt green fronds of salt-sea breeze
Creep across curving shingle and shell
Mingle with voices at play in the quay
And dance in the caress of the quickening swell.

I am thrall'd therefore so easily
Lying, washed over, in constant sea.

-- Caroline Boon

Caroline Boon introduces 'In Constancy'

The first thing that struck me when I was sitting in the workshop was the sound of the words as we circled round the room reading them from our lists. With the theme of the sea, I had the idea that I wanted to make my sonnet sound like the sea. I experimented with lots of words which had a hushed 's' sound, and I managed to produce a few lines using only these words. However, the main problem occurred when trying to fit them into a regular sonnet rhyme scheme, and I eventually abandoned this idea altogether. The words that I used in my poem here, such as 'silky' 'starfish' 'sounds' 'salt-sea' 'shingle' and 'shell' are all remnants of my original intention.

When discussing my poem in the second session, Lucy pointed out that I had used many tropes in the poem, such as 'through yonder window breaks' and 'pregnant dawn'. I imagined the speaker of the poem lying in bed with the window open and a sea view beyond. I wanted to capture the feeling when one first awakes of everything being perfect for a moment. Feeling unable to articulate this perfection for myself, I think this is the reason why I (subconsciously) turned to trope.

The other feeling that I wanted to create was a sense of the ambiguity of language. The title 'In Constancy' can mean either 'inconstancy' (i.e. not constant), 'in constancy' (i.e. constant), or, if you hear it read, 'in constant sea' or 'inconstant sea'. I wanted the reader to decide how to read and understand the title for themselves. Similarly, in the final lines 'lying' can mean either *lying* in bed or not telling the truth. The meaning one attributes to 'lying' determines to some extend how one understands and interprets the title, and perhaps the poem itself.

When the speaker first awakes the morning is 'silky' and the waves are 'white'; both intimate images of perfection. Yet as a consciousness of the world overcomes the initial sleepiness, the tone shifts slightly. As the light 'breaks' through the window, so the sense of perfection 'breaks'. I wanted the sea view to subtly offer a story; thus the fishermen 'trawling' the sea, 'voices at play' and 'dancing' in a 'caress' imply a rendezvous between lovers and the images of 'guarding' and 'green' suggest jealousy. Finally the saltiness conveys bitterness whilst the sea itself is continually changing with the tide. Therefore, nothing is constant, and one can both *lie* and lie in bed.

Jenny Lewis writes a critical analysis

Caroline uses a play on the word 'inconstancy' to suggest the mutability of relationships which is echoed by the constant ebb and flow of the sea. The reference to *Romeo and Juliet* in line two re-enforces the inter-textual nature of the poem as does the allusion to Donne's *Selfe Love* in 'thrall'd' (line 13). The invocation of Shakespeare's doomed lovers adds a note of sharpness to the lyricism of the poem, and this is bolstered later by the repetition of 'salt green fronds' and 'salt-sea breeze.' Salt is used to add savour, but it can also be rubbed into wounds. The sub-text, it seems, is that the speaker is overcome by mixed emotions, it is as if she is lying helpless in the foam on the shoreline, swayed to and fro by feeling. She is 'Lying' in the sea, lying down on the strand, but she could also be evading, or concealing truth – possibly from herself. This ambiguity is developed further as we sense her mixed reaction to being 'thrall'd'. Here Caroline is exploring the paradox of love and, indeed, Donne's use of paradox in lines such as 'To enter in these bonds is to be free', from *Elegie XIX: To His Mistress Going to Bed* and, from *Holy Sonnet XIV* :

> Take me to you, imprison me, for I
> Except you' enthrall me never shall be free

are similarly exploring the complex nature of the tension between innocence and experience, sacred and profane love. Also present is the Renaissance idea of the masochistic lover, reluctantly overwhelmed by love.

Overlaying the density of the allusions, the octave and first four lines of the sestet build a luminous structure of sense-related images: 'Silky starfish light', 'Rushing sounds of foamy white/Waves' 'pearly rays', 'hastening glow', 'the caress of the quickening swell'. The alliterating 's' and 'sh' sounds mimic the sound of the sea. Appropriately for such an allusive poem, the poet has used the Shakespearean sonnet form – ABAB, CDCD, EFEF, GG. The first four lines alternate iambic pentameter with iambic tetrameter. This becomes looser as the sonnet progresses and the lines lengthen. The uneven line lengths suggest, again, the ebb and flow of the ocean on the shoreline.

The weightiness of the allusive imagery combined with the more contemporary language of the group 'word pool' sets up an interesting dynamic, although the archaisms of 'yonder' and 'thrall'd' have a slightly grounding effect on the otherwise fluid rhythms of the sonnet.

Lucy Newlyn edits

WAKING

Silky morning
starfish light
breaks through.

Fishing boats
trawl the morn,
guarding their hoard

in the quickening glow.
Green fronds
of salt-sea breeze

creep across
curving shingle
and shell,

mingle with voices
at play in the quay,
dance in the swell.

-- Lucy Newlyn (after Caroline Boon)

Note: I thought that the purely descriptive parts of Caroline's poem were delicate and beautiful. I wanted to show how effective they could be, just standing on their own, as a list of images. I have removed the allusions, archaisms and poetic tropes as well as the pun 'constant sea/constancy' and the presence of a complicating subjectivity. I have kept one rhyme, shell/swell, and moved it into a prominent position at the close of the poem. I have also replaced 'hastening' with the word 'quickening' (which occurs later in Caroline's poem) because the verb 'hasten' is too archaic for my taste. Caroline's poem was in the style of the Elizabethans and Metaphysicals; my adaptation is Imagist.

Elizabeth Scott-Baumann edits

IN CONSTANCY

Silky morning
Starfish light
Through yonder window breaks

Rushing sounds
Foamy white
Waves greet me as I wake

Pearly rays
Pregnant dawn
Give birth to a heaving crescendo

Salt green fronds
Salt-sea breeze
Mounted by fishing boats trawling the morn

Curving shells
Creeping shingle
Guarding their hoard in the hastening glow.

Mingling voices
Play in the quay
And dance in the caress of the quickening swell.

I am thrall'd therefore so easily
Lying, washed over, in constant sea.

-- Elizabeth Scott-Baumann

Note: Caroline used several richly evocative descriptive phrases composed 'adjective – noun of adjective – noun', e.g. 'Rushing sounds of foamy white', 'pearly rays of pregnant dawn', 'salt green fronds of salt-sea breeze'. In order to create a slightly less ordered impression, more like experience when you are half asleep, or fragments of light coming through a curtain, I divided these phrases into their two parts, to create a structure of six stanzas and a couplet. I think the gentleness of these slightly dislocated sensual impressions gives the final couplet more impact, as a sharply articulated conclusion.

Alice Wood

SONNET

Of all the silky pearly-twirly opals,
You the chosen are my pocket one.
My private echo, your reassurance lulls;
Your promises swing every jibe to run.
But who are you to promise me the ocean,
So I believe of horses that you tell?
At best to leave me sickened by the motion;
At worst to leave one bulbous as the swell.
And who am I to keep you in my pocket?
To snare you with the whispers that you voice?
To form with fears and doubts a cutting locket –
Why do we all entwine ourselves by choice?!
Yet I know your ridges worn by waves and weather;
It was they that moulded hope we'd wear together.

-- Alice Wood

Alice Wood introduces 'Of all the silky, pearly-twirly opals'

When I began the poem I was more concerned with conveying images that had come to me during the word association exercise than with writing in strict form. After I had found some shape to my ideas I then concentrated on trying to use them to construct a Shakespearean sonnet, but all the time I was focused on content. I wanted the two opposing lines of thought in the speaker's head to run backwards and forwards in phases like waves ebbing and flowing, and I concentrated on creating these two opposing feelings. I am pleased with the effect of these, but should have paid more attention to the form to create a stronger poem.

Caroline Boon writes a critical analysis

Alice's interpretation of the sea theme consists in the treasuring of a shell that the speaker has found. Words such as 'the chosen' and 'my private' suggest both ownership and intimacy. However, the speaker's relationship with the shell appears to shift after the fourth line, and despite her ownership of it, it seems to have control over her emotions. She seems caught between the 'promise' of the shell and her right to keep it for herself. 'And who am I to keep you in my pocket?' she asks, yet the 'fears and doubts' two lines later are her own, not the shell's, and the image of 'entwining' oneself suggests that really it is she who wants freedom from the shell rather than a call from the shell for its release. The 'cutting locket' suggests that she feels she must keep the shell close, even though she is aware that it is hurting her emotionally.

The sonnet's metre echoes the speaker's dilemma over the shell. The irregular metre is in stark contrast to the regular Shakespearean rhyming scheme of ABAB, CDCD, EFEF, GG. Therefore the comfort of choosing and ownership seems held in the smooth, steady rhyming scheme. It suggests an appearance of perfection upon the surface. Yet the metre, which seems to resist regularity in any form, matches the inner turmoil of the speaker, finding the shell alternately precious and painful.

Her first line is in iambic pentameter, with a hypercatalectic foot. This is followed by a shorter, nine syllabic line in trochaic metre, with a catalectic foot. Her choice of metre in these two lines allows a strong emphasis on 'you' at the beginning of the second line. Because the longer, first line is compensated for by the shorter, second line, the metre is harmonised to form one sentence. This harmony is mirrored in the theme of the sentence, which is the speaker's declaration of ownership of the shell. Alice's metre also anticipates her punctuation, as can be seen in the third line, where two unstressed syllables fall either side of a comma, almost like the echo itself. Alice also uses stress in the metre in the fifth line to emphasise the central players in her poem, 'who' 'you' and 'me'.

The line 'your promises swing every jibe to run' reminds me of a sailing boat. The words 'swing' 'jibe' and 'run' can all be used to describe a boat with the wind in her sails. A 'jibe' is sailing terminology for a sailing boat turning and changing the direction it is sailing in. A result of the turn is the sail flipping round to the other side of the boat and the wind filling the sail from the other side. The nature of a 'jibe' in sailing is that it is very quick and the metre here captures the speed of the manoeuvre. The subtle use of sailing terminology, describing a boat changing tack, anticipates the shift in tone in Alice's poem and the movement from the speaker's ownership of the shell to the control the shell has over the owner's emotions.

The poem's final couplet maintains the sense of ambiguity that has been sustained throughout. Alice uses both 'worn' and 'wear' in the two lines respectively. The verb is ambiguous, because it can mean 'to put on' as one *wears* clothes, or a constant 'rubbing' or *wearing* away. The 'moulded hope we'd wear together' can be understood in terms of the speaker 'wearing' the hope as she wears the cutting locket but also as hope wearing away. This final interpretation leaves one with the impression that the relationship is ultimately wearing them both down, just as the motion of the sea wears down the objects within it.

Caroline Boon edits

SONNET

Of all the silky pearly-twirly opals,
You the chosen are my pocket one.
My private echo, your reassurance lulls;
But who am I to keep you in my pocket?
To snare you with the whispers that you voice?
And who are you to promise me the ocean,
To form with fears and doubts a cutting locket –
At best to leave me sickened by the motion;
At worst to leave one bulbous as the swell.
Yet I know your ridges worn by waves and weather;
Moulded hope we'd wear together.
Of all the silky pearly-twirly opals,
You the chosen are my pocket one.

-- Caroline Boon (after Alice Wood)

NOTE: I liked Alice's use of rhetoric, and rearranged her poem to impress more deeply the sense of question and answer in her poem. I loved the first two lines and wanted them to echo even after the poem had ended, hence the repeated couplet.

Lucy Newlyn edits

CHOSEN

Of all the silky pearly-twirly opals,
You the chosen are my pocket one

your pocket one.
But who are you to keep me in your pocket?

My private echo, your reassurance lulls,
For you the chosen are my pocket one

your pocket one.
But who are you to snare me with your voice?

Your ridges worn by waves and weather
moulded the hope we'd wear together,

for you the chosen are my pocket one.
Your pocket one.

But who am I to promise you the ocean?
Promise me the ocean.

For you the chosen are my pocket one.

-- Lucy Newlyn (after Alice Wood)

Note: I found Alice's opening lines very arresting, and thought the second might make an interesting refrain. I also wanted to emphasise the insistent self-interrogation – the swinging backwards and forwards of doubts and anxieties – which provide the central structural principle in her sonnet. Playing on the idea of voice and echo (which enters her poem at line 3), I turned her poem into a sequence of questions and answers. I tried to suggest an ambiguity about who it is that is speaking – the shell, a lover, or an internal voice – by playing games with the pronouns and reversing expectations at the end. I also wanted the echoic device to suggest the sound of waves advancing and retreating on the shore.

Daniel Harkin

CHORAL

Somebody locked your voice into my shell –
Rough ridges constricting curving tubes;
Unexploded. Leviathans and truths
Pouting ribbed lip swallowed gestalt of swells
Souls that claw and tempest-tear, stories to tell.
Below sheer insurmountable, frothy hooves
Fringe leathery impenetrable that heaves,
Pressing on surfacing screams from those who fell.
Net tight on tantrums of soda and colours
Extrinsic expanse held by tawny, tortoise prison.
Rousing rising spewing seeding beyond reach.
Wrecks, rapes and visions far from prying fingers
Where gallops foam and hides the horizon
Your surface this exile can't hope to breach.

-- Daniel Harkin

Daniel Harkin introduces 'Choral'

I wanted to write about the feelings I have towards democracy. The oceans with all their variety of live, violence beauty and unpredictable nature, open to the influence of the environment, seemed the perfect thing to discuss my feelings. My position in relation to the sea, separated, on land, also helped me understand where I tend to position myself in relation to other people. Being somewhat academic in a working-class environment, then being a working-class boy in a middle-class world leaves me feeling a bit lost because I know there are great chunks of me I can't share with a large number of people. That's why the poetic persona loses his possession by the end of the sonnet and becomes an exile not an individual.

I tried to create a collection of sounds, more than anything. Having a myriad collection of words made me decide to jumble up a lot of them to create patterns, sounds and rhythms. The idea was that I'd use half rhyme and pararhyme, partly because I'm fascinated by the likes of Owen and Britten who make music from discord; also because I wanted to suppress the form, which is why I avoided the more comfortable Shakespearean sonnet. The shell is an imperfect prison for something as awesome as the sea. I tried to suggest the imperfect framing and my detached feelings towards everyone else through the opening and closing lines.

I started to arrange sentences through word-patterning, alliteration, assonance, internal rhyme. The use of words like 'impenetrable' and 'insurmountable' was to add eddies. 'Leviathans' because they were the beasts of chaos in Jewish mythology. I used a few trochees because I felt the cadence helped reproduce the swell and ebb of the tide and a sense of disappointment. The sonnet is supposed to mimic the fall from a cliff ('Below sheer insurmountable') as someone drowns ('Pressing on surfacing screams from those who feel'). This is also my customary reference to Peake's Fuchsia. The 'camera' (my imagination works cinematically) plunges down and then surfaces to take in the expanse of sea and horizon, all within a shell.

I tried to capture the idea that the ocean does end, it has fringes where it frays and yet these fringes have great power, reshaping the land. Thus the images of ‘frothy hooves’ and ‘gallops foam’. Someone mentioned horses in the word-storm session and I have a similar relationship to horses as I do the sea and democracy – so it all went in to the cacophonic mix! I tried to capture this in the title choral/coral, trying to make the sea a collective thing rather than a singular identity, which is what makes it so powerful, unsettling, unstable.

I’m not convinced that my sonnet was in any way successful. As ever with the things I write, its theme is made obscure by my indulgence in vocabulary. The use of ‘leathery’, for instance, was after seeing the sea at night on holiday in Cornwall: it looked like the hide of a great reptile, breathing. By trying to create an orgiastic cacophony of sound and rhythm I neglected some other, more fundamental things. In spite of that, I’m glad to get socialist prejudice towards the masses out of my system.

Alice Wood writes a critical analysis

In ‘Choral’, Daniel emphasises the power of the sea. This power is symbolic of an oppressive tyranny, as he indicates with his usage in line 4 of the word ‘Leviathans’, meaning both a sea monster and an autocratic monster. The poem focuses on the image of the shell as a method of imprisonment. The sonnet is Petrarchan, with the circularity that the repetition creates, similarly constricting the reader in the poem with rhyme.

The first and last lines of the poem stand out as they are written as ordinary speech; both grammatically correct with a conversational rhythm. They have a detached tone, which gives a suppressed beginning and end to the poem, in contrast to the emotive response in the middle section of the poem, characterised by an overload of adjectives and a lack of conventional, coherent sentence structures. The underlying metre of the poem is iambic, but it is continually counterpointed by trochaic, dactylic and spondaic feet which effectively evoke the raging tumult of the sea in lines 2-13, enhanced by the unconventional word order. The alliteration throughout the central body of the poem, particularly in lines 2, 4, 10 and 11 emphasises the constriction that the sonnet focuses on. The compound 'tempest-tear' in line 5 suggests the fury and turbulence of the souls by means of sea imagery, with reference also to the mental turbulence that the characters suffer in Shakespeare's *The Tempest*. Daniel's use of half-rhyme, with 'tubes/truths' and 'hooves/heaves', also adds to the turbulence of the poem, by preventing the imprisoning rhymes that the Petrarchan form creates, from causing the poem to be static. The dash that ends the first line marks its break with the line that follows and this middle section. The last line of the poem seems to follow on from this dash.

The first and last lines create an abstract for the poem. The first line reveals the situation of oppression that is continually presented throughout the octet, while the last line concludes the hopelessness of the situation that the sestet presents. Lines 12-13 build towards the anticlimax of the last line with a trochaic rhythm pulling the reader forward with a sense of hope and of the struggle of the oppressed voices of the sea. The struggle is unfulfilled however, as the last line breaks from the speed of this rhythm, moving back to an iambic metre with the suggestion of dactylic feet to give a sense of continuity. The last line returns to the suppressed tone of the first line, ending the sonnet on a note of despair for those lost to the autocratic sea monster that the poem describes.

Elizabeth Scott-Baumann edits

CHORAL

Somebody locked your voice into my shell –
Rough ridges constricting curving tubes;
Unexploded.

Leviathans and truths pouting
Ribbed lip swallowed gestalt of swells
Stories to tell.

Below sheer insurmountable, frothy hooves
Pressing on surfacing screams from those who fell.
On tantrums.

Extrinsic expanse held by tawny, tortoise prison.
Rousing rising spewing seeding
Beyond reach.

Wrecks, rapes and visions far from prying fingers
Where gallops foam and hides the horizon

Your surface this exile can't hope to breach.

-- Elizabeth Scott-Baumann (after Daniel Harkin)

Note: I have tried to reinforce the theme I took from this poem by making each stanza end with an expression of inarticulacy. This inability to speak is finally articulated in the last line.

Caroline Boon edits

CHORAL

Rough ridges constricting curving tubes;
Unexploded. Leviathans and truths
Pouting ribbed lip swallowed gestalt of swells
Souls that claw and tempest-tear,
Below sheer insurmountable, frothy hooves
Pressing on surfacing screams from those who fell.
Net tight tantrums of soda and colour
Rising, spewing, seeding beyond reach.
Where foam gallops and hides the horizon
Extrinsic expanse held by tawny, tortoise prison.
Somebody locked your voice into my shell.

-- Caroline Boon (after Daniel Harkin)

NOTE: This poem was particularly hard to edit. Looking back now I think I still prefer the original! However I disliked the way the original ended – I felt it was not strong enough to do justice to the violent imagery.

I found the original first line very haunting and this is the reason I inserted it at the end here.

Lucy Newlyn edits

LEVIATHAN

Somebody locked your voice
into my shell:
rough ridges constricting curving tubes,
souls that claw and tempest-tear
at pouting ribbed-lip swell.

Somebody locked your voice
into my shell:
below sheer insurmountable,
hooves stamping on screams
from those who fell.

Somebody locked your voice
into my shell:
Net-tight tantrums seeding beyond reach,
far from the horizon
exile cannot breach.

Somebody locked your voice
into my shell:
the leathery hide of a great reptile
breathing; Leviathans and truths,
stories to tell.

-- Lucy Newlyn (after Daniel Harkin)

Note: I found the syntax of Daniel's sonnet difficult to follow, and wanted to simplify it; so I cut out all the sub-clauses I did not understand, aiming for a clearer progression of thought. Daniel's opening line worked very well. I kept that as a refrain, using it to structure the pile-up of nightmare images. I retained the 'ell' rhymes and thus created cycles within the poem: I hoped that the ghost-rhyme with 'hell' would evoke the obsessional atmosphere of the original. I introduced one completely new line: 'the leathery hide of a great reptile/breathing'. This graphic image comes directly from Daniel's introduction to his sonnet, where he uses it to describe the Cornish coastline seen by night. I think it connects with his mention of the sea-monster Leviathan. I have moved Leviathan into the title so as to give it greater prominence.

Putting Practice into Theory

by Lucy Newlyn

The workshops created a uniquely enabling environment, in which it was possible to cross the creative/critical divide in both directions. By setting up the experiment in six different stages, we were able to observe the nature of these crossings, their effects on the writing and reading processes, and the responses of those involved.

Looking back on the whole process, it is possible to see each of its separate stages as an exploration of questions fundamental to literary theory. Through the practice of collaborative and individual writing, we had investigated such topics as authorial intention, reader-response, ownership of texts, canon-formation, intertextuality, and the anxiety of influence/reception. Because the process was not theory-led, these topics arose incidentally. This made them more approachable, of more immediate consequence, and more readily understood.

Having observed the ways in which practice can enlighten theoretical issues, I have become convinced that creative writing could usefully be integrated into the teaching of elementary literary theory, as well as critical analysis. What follows is an attempt to clarify the questions that were raised at each stage of the creative/critical process, and why they are significant outside their immediate context.

Stage One: Collaborative Writing

Our first workshop established the conditions we needed for uninhibited creative writing. We wrote down our responses to the trigger-words at high speed. Doing so with everyone in the room together gave the activity a compelling sense of collaborative immediacy. It would be difficult to generate the same atmosphere under different conditions. Although the process was quite intimidating to start with, we soon got used to the loss of inhibition involved. Responding spontaneously to our chosen theme, without any screening or blocking of the words we jotted down, made us all curious about what would be revealed, in ourselves and in other members of the group.

As we each read aloud our word-associations, we noticed overlapping thematic preoccupations among group members, but also the unique slant provided by each individual's imagination. Jenny and I had chosen the sea as our theme partly because we were interested in seeing how the group would respond to elemental subject-matter: the sea has a universal appeal, and has been connected by poets through the ages with vast subjects, such as time, memory, loss, and the unconscious. Some would argue that, in recording the overlapping word-associations of the group, we were drawing on what Jung called the 'collective unconscious'. But it is equally arguable that we were tapping into a reservoir of *accumulated cultural associations*, many of which came to this particular group via our shared resource, the English poetic canon. Brendan Jones, an American student, drew on a distinctively American ideolect, which barely touched the associations shared by other group members. This confirmed that the associative process is culturally inflected. It follows that a more culturally diverse group would produce a wider range of associations.

The group's editing process provided a rare opportunity for observing how a critical consensus can be reached, even on a question so arbitrary and personal as which words sound better among a given list. Past experience had taught me that it is difficult to reach consensus in matters of taste. So I was surprised at the swiftness and confidence with which, jointly, we arrived at our judgement of which words to select for the group poem. Why is it that some words were instantly liked by all members of the group, and others were felt to be less rich, less suggestive, less appropriate? Would agreement have been reached so easily if we had introduced greater cultural diversity?

Perhaps the fact that most members of the group were already accustomed to working together played its part. A tightly-knit group of readers specialising in English literature, we formed a readily identifiable 'interpretive community', to use a term coined by the literary theorist Stanley Fish. With the exception of Brendan (and another American, Charlene Dy, who joined us for later sessions) we were all English, with various prejudices, tastes, and reading-practices in common.

Roughly speaking, our interpretive community shared the same 'horizon of expectations': a term used by the reception theorist Robert Jauss to define the climate of opinion in which a text may expect to be received. The fact that we were straying outside our usual academic territory made us adjust and re-formulate some of our rules and assumptions during the editorial process. What we achieved by drawing up our 'shortlist' of words was a clearer definition of our horizon of expectations. In a sense, we were anticipating and preparing ourselves for the future reception of our poems by the group.

As the process of group-editing gathered momentum, it is possible that we began to choose words as much for their connectiveness with preceding and following words, as for their innate richness. We worked so fast that we were not conscious of shaping a connective thread between the words. But already we could see and hear how an individual's words, as selected by the group, could hold together into a meaningful word-cluster. I remember noticing how richly suggestive 'salt, rough, history' looked; and also that the words *sounded* better the other way round: 'rough, salt, history'.

Wolfgang Iser, the most influential reader-response theorist of the twentieth century, argued that an important early stage in understanding a text is filling in its 'gaps'. We understand a text, he claimed, by processing it as a continuum. As we encounter gaps, inconsistencies or blockages in the text, we assess them and make them fit as best they can into a thread which links them with what comes before and after. As he puts it, in his essay 'The reading process: a phenomenological approach': 'whenever the flow is interrupted and we are led off in unexpected directions, the opportunity is always given to us to bring into play our own faculty for establishing connections – for filling the gaps left by the text itself'. This process of consistency building is one of the basic tools a reader has. It is also, of course, a writer's tool. In our workshop activity, we were already beginning to use this tool, as reader-writers, in the assemblage of our group-poem. Individual word-clusters provided the basic units of meaning.

When we had arrived at our edited word-pool, we could see how our own word-associations worked alongside others. The 'Group Poem' we had generated seemed to come from a kind of creative tension between the word-clusters in each line, and the onward movement provided by thematic consistency. Of course, because so many reader-writers were involved, there were still 'gaps' which needed to be filled in order to make a meaningful whole. And there were as many possible meaningful wholes as there were writer-readers participating in the workshop. For, as Iser puts it,

> one text is potentially capable of several different realisations, and no reading can ever exhaust the full potential, for each individual will fill in the gaps in his own way, thereby excluding the other possibilities; as he reads he will make his own decision as to how the gap is to be filled. In this very act the dynamics of reading are revealed.

Stage Two: Individual Writing

In prospect, making a poem from the word-pool seemed an artificial activity: a bit like trying to make do with the pre-selected words that come in a Fridge Magnet Poetry kit. But it worked very well as a means of triggering the writing process, and proved unexpectedly rewarding. Tracing connective threads between different words or word-clusters was a bit like making moats round several sand-castles, then connecting up the moats and watching the water trickle round. There was a combined sense of freedom and discipline in sticking as much as possible to words from the pool: freedom, because so many of the associations came from outside our own imaginations; and discipline, because the group pool set its own parameters round the growth of our poems.

Participants were free to draw not only on the edited word pool, but on words that had been rejected during the group editorial process; and most of us did so. Was this simply to increase our choice of vocabulary, or were we consciously slanting our own contributions away from the consensus view? What was the ratio of competitive to collaborative endeavour, at this stage in the experiment? Was there any component of what Harold Bloom called 'the anxiety of influence' in our word choices?

Bloom argued that the greatness of predecessors is a source of anxiety to poets, who negotiate their own poetic identity under the shadow of what has been achieved before. To arrive at their own voice, they have to clear imaginative space for themselves by battling with their precursors. Originality can only be achieved by avoiding or transcending what has gone before. The anxiety of influence can be felt in relation to contemporaries as well as predecessors. Were any of us, consciously or unconsciously, avoiding the poems in the word-pool because we hoped to transcend them?

Writing poetry is normally a solitary activity; but during our experiment it proved otherwise. Drawing on the word-pool for words and images in our own poems felt like an extension of the shared act of pooling the words in the workshop. We knew we would strike a chord with someone in the group every time we drew a word from the pool. A kind of sympathy, or sense of community, between writer and reader/listener was already established, even before reading aloud to the group; and this made the activity of writing feel less closed-off, less solipsistic. Similarly, when hearing other people's poems read aloud, there was a sense of enjoyment that came from noticing the words or images we ourselves had contributed. Hearing 'our own' words in their new contexts gave a strange sense of being dissociated, almost alienated, from our feelings and ideas. This feeling came close to the effect described by the Russian formalists as *de-familiarisation.* The importance of this feeling/effect to our project was twofold: firstly, it allowed us all to see that there can be a flexible negotiation between individual and group identity; and secondly, it enabled each of us to achieve a distance from our own imaginative processes. Writing something and then standing back from it to evaluate its quality entails making part of oneself *im*personal. Hearing how someone else handles the same words in different ways enhances one's ability to achieve this critical distance, this impersonality.

Stage Three: Collaborative Criticism

Over the years, Jenny has evolved a special method in her creative writing courses, for awakening shared creative energy. By enabling participants to draw on a common word-pool, and then feed their individual contributions back into the group, she has found an ideal way of enabling the balance between individual and shared creative activity. Because of her experience, she was very familiar with the excitement which a group working well together can generate, especially at the stage when individuals return to the group with their finished poems. But for an apprentice like myself, the experience was still relatively new; and it is impossible to describe the anticipation and pleasure I derived from the workshop sessions in which we read our poems aloud. It was as though the oral tradition of poetry had been re-awakened.

The only thing I have heard that is remotely comparable is a session of Irish fiddle music: one person starts up with a well-known tune, gives it a particular twist by adding personal variations, then passes it on, almost like a runner in a relay-race, to the next fiddler. Each fiddler takes a turn in modifying the tune, and so on until one of the fiddlers links the old tune into an entirely new one, and the cycle begins again. The essential thing with fiddle music (or indeed the folk tradition), is that it is always moving, always adding to or modifying something familiar. In our workshop, the conditions were similar because all our poems drew on a fund of common words and images, to which by this stage we had become accustomed. What we heard, when each person read their poems aloud, was an individual's transformation of communal material. There was a sense of tapping into something shared, yet this was overlaid by the poet's new and unique voice.

T.S. Eliot argued that poetry involves a fusion between 'tradition' and 'individual talent'. A poet's voice is never purely personal. Voices from the past speak in and through the language he chooses. Every poetic utterance draws from a vast cultural reservoir of words, metaphors, images, myths, motifs. Poetry is thus a kind of remembering, in which the present constantly honours and re-vivifies the past. As he puts it, in his most famous essay, “Tradition and the Individual Talent”,

> The historical sense involves a perception, not only of the pastness of the past, but of its presence; the historical sense compels a man to write not merely with his own generation in his bones, but with a feeling that the whole of the literature of Europe from Homer and within it the whole of the literature of his own country has a simultaneous existence and composes a similar order.

Eliot’s model of authorship was consciously fashioned as an alternative to the Romantics’. Eliot overturned the individualist emphasis on originality (which had grown out of a competitive preoccupation with the ownership of texts), replacing it with ideas of anonymity and communality. Writing, he said, involved ‘a continual self-sacrifice, a continual extinction of personality….Poetry is not a turning loose of emotion, but an escape from emotion; it is not the expression of personality, but an escape from personality’.

It might be helpful to think of our poetry workshop as a microcosm of the processes Eliot had in mind, with each finished sonnet representing a fusion of the individual and the communal. But is the Romantic idea of authorship so easily discarded? Even as one observes the common fund of imagery which holds all our sonnets together, one is also aware of the distinctiveness of each participant’s voice. It is almost as if there is a tug-of-war going on, between the individual and the communal. Bloom’s idea of the anxious poet begins to re-surface once again.

In setting up our experiment, Jenny and I consciously wanted to encourage a communal or collaborative model of poetry: this is primarily what the workshop conditions are for. It was therefore intriguing to notice how an alternative model began to emerge as time went on. For instance, we were not very far into our second workshop before we were discussing publication of our sonnets. This raised questions about the ownership of poems generated by the group. If participants wanted to publish their poems as their own, did they really have the right to do so? At what point did a joint endeavour cross over into a single one? If the word pool was the group’s property, did this mean that the group also owned each separate line? And what of the finished sonnets? Who 'owned' them? Our discussion ended in a diplomatic compromise between competitive and collaborative models of authorship. If any of our sonnets were published, they should be over a single name, but with an acknowledgement of the St Edmund Hall workshop.

Discussing the poems at our second workshop brought into focus differences in the way that each participant had handled both the theme of the sea and the sonnet form. At this stage in the workshop process, we were eager to hear constructive criticism of our own work, but we were also wary of evaluating the quality of work produced by others. Perhaps the struggle to create the sonnets had made us sensitive to the flaws in what we ourselves had written, so we held back in our criticism. Discussion focused on the content and form of the sonnets: we delayed our evaluative judgements until a later stage in the experiment.

When planning how to conduct this second workshop, Jenny and I had agreed that we wanted to bring into focus the clashes that can occur between authorial intention and reader response. The workshop confirmed that texts can generate a multiplicity of meanings. Every participant had a slightly different view of each poem we discussed, and sometimes there was a striking difference between what the author had intended and how he or she was read.

We had all expected this, because our experience in critical analysis classes (and our knowledge of literary theory) had taught us that there is a great deal more to a poem's meaning than what the author intended. Unconscious meanings aside, there are multiple latent meanings, which only become realised as the text is read and re-read; for the reader is always in a collaborative relation to the text. What we could not anticipate was how participants would feel, as writers whose control over their own poems was relinquished the moment they read their poems aloud. The responses were various. Ben Burton, an experienced writer (but unaccustomed to workshop conditions) confessed that he felt wary of the process, and was surprised by the intensity of his own concern to correct 'false' readings. In no part of his coursework had he become so vividly aware of what Roland Barthes meant when he announced that 'the birth of the reader must be at the cost of the death of the author'. In responding like this, Ben gave voice to what I have elsewhere called an 'anxiety of reception'. This is the reverse of Bloom's 'anxiety of influence': it is an anxiety that authors feel in relation to their readers, rather than their predecessors. It can take many forms, and it frequently gives rise to defensive strategies, designed to control and direct reader-response. A poet who writes prefaces or notes to the reader may well be dealing with an 'anxiety of reception'.

Brendan felt very differently from Ben. Having attended poetry workshops in the States, he was accustomed to the feedback stage in the creative process, and positively welcomed the discovery of meanings he had not intended. Brendan's preference was for the kind of poetry that held itself open to as many readings as possible. He explained that this was why he had chosen to write an un-punctuated sonnet, thus enabling the syntax to flow in several different directions. The term used in Anglo-Saxon poetry, for a line which can be read syntactically in different ways is apo-koinu; and several members of the group observed that Brendan had used this ancient poetic technique.

Roland Barthes saw texts as either 'writerly' or 'readerly'. A writerly text is one which invites the reader to become just as active as the writer, and capable of the same creativity. The opposite of a 'writerly' text, in Barthes' formulation, is a 'readerly' text, in which the reader is required to submit passively to authorial manipulation. The novelist and theorist Umberto Eco coincided in some respect with Barthes. He believed that texts were 'open' or 'closed', depending on the degree of reader-response they elicited through various textual and extra-textual or para-textual markers. Brendan's poem would be a good example of a 'writerly' text as described by Barthes, or of an 'open' text as Eco defines it.

Or would it?

At a later workshop, I challenged Brendan about whether his poem was really as 'writerly' or 'open' as it seems. He claimed that, in each new reading of his sonnet a different version of the poem's syntax would be achieved. I disagreed: it seems to me that, when reading the poem aloud, we become aware of what Chomsky would call the 'deep structure' of its syntax, which turns out to be quite orthodox. Even without punctuation, we pause in the places where a comma might be expected, and we control our breathing so as enable a meaningful inflection of the words on the page. Caroline Boon's later editing of Brendan's sonnet used line-endings to supply the orthodox syntax which he had suppressed. My own editing of the poem differs little from Caroline's in its reading of the syntax.

I think Brendan's poem might best be described as a 'closed' text which he has disguised as an 'open' one. One way of testing this out would be to ask twenty readers to supply missing punctuation, and see whether consensus could be reached.

Stage Four: Individual Criticism

This was the stage in our experiment for which we were most prepared, because all of us have had a great deal of practice in writing critical analyses of poems. And yet even here something quite new was involved. For in this case the poem was not part of the English canon, and composed several hundred years ago; but written the previous week by a colleague, a friend, a student, or a tutor. Did our personal knowledge of each other affect the analytical process? Did the dynamic of our partnership, or the communal circumstances of production, influence the way in which we wrote about each other's poems?

The answer to the first question is far from straightforward. So far as technique was concerned, we treated the activity of critical analysis in much the same way as we would have done, had the poem been by Wordsworth, or Shelley, or Plath. And yet, because we all knew each other well (at least by comparison with those authors), there was inevitably a level of readerly understanding already in place, before critical analysis began.

Normally, critics use whatever biographical or historical knowledge they can get hold of to arrive at a preliminary inroad into a given text. Even candidates taking a 'Critical Analysis' paper in their first year exams make use of knowledge outside the text to interpret what is in it. If one possesses extra-textual knowledge of any kind, being asked to discount it poses a challenge which feels counter-intuitive; and it is this that makes a purely formalist approach to critical analysis so artificial. Indeed, one could argue that there can be no such thing as a purely formalist approach to critical analysis, unless one introduces complete anonymity into the process. Even just knowing the name of the author or the date of a text's composition introduces all kinds of extra-textual influences on the act of interpretation.

The critical analysis stage in our experiment challenged us by reversing our accustomed position *vis-à-vis* biographical knowledge of our subject-matter. In effect, we knew too much: far from looking for possible interpretive inroads into our material, we were more or less bound to read in a certain way because of what we knew. The poems were, in short, *overdetermined.* As Elizabeth Scott-Baumann put it, 'I found myself consciously trying to exclude personal knowledge of the poet when analysing his/her work. The workshop forced me to objectify my critical analysis skills in the very context in which I could be most subjective'.

The answer to the second question is easier. Coming to the act of critical analysis fresh from our own struggles with writing sonnets, there is no doubt that our practical experience fed into the way we wrote about the achievements of our partners. This increased our enjoyment of how they had handled the sonnet form, and it also sharpened our ability to comment on how they had achieved certain poetic effects. In addition to this, there was the incidental pleasure of noticing where we had coincided with our partners in the choice of words or word-clusters from the group pool. For instance, Jenny had made much more of the phrase 'rough salt history' than I had, by moving it to the beginning of her poem. I remember noticing how she had made the power of that phrase resonate through her whole sonnet. I don't think I would have observed this so sharply, had I not made a different use of the same phrase.

Stage Five: Editing

One of the most enjoyable stages in our experiment came right at the end, when we edited each other's poems. Here, by the act of re-writing, we were allowing ourselves to be uninhibited in our judgements and preferences. Remembering the collaboration of T.S. Eliot and Ezra Pound gave us the opportunity to think of editing as a creative activity in its own right, like translating.

Eliot's *The Wasteland* is the most famous example in our language of creative editing. The poem as we know it would not have existed had it not been for the intervention of Pound, who cut vast expanses of the poem as originally conceived. In acknowledgement of his debt to Pound, Eliot dedicated the published poem to his friend, with the Italian epigraph, 'il miglior fabbro', meaning 'the better maker'. This was a generous act, welcoming in a spirit of collaboration the decisiveness of an acute critic. In a sense, Eliot was thereby defining Pound as his 'ideal reader'. It is not often that ideal readers are also actual ones – indeed Wolfgang Iser, who coined the terminology, would argue that they are by definition distinct. But literary collaborations, such as those of Wordsworth and Coleridge, Eliot and Pound, or Edward Thomas and Robert Frost, enable one to see the possible overlapping (or conflation) of the ideal and the actual.

Some of us consciously took Pound as our role-model in the editing process. I remember the great pleasure I derived from discarding the titles of all the poems I was editing, and also from getting rid of the allusions and archaic diction in Caroline's and Ben's sonnets. Moving out of the sonnet structure into less structured forms allowed me to bring out different thematic emphases. In several cases I used triplets, which is the form I use most naturally, so it really seemed as if I was making these poems my own. The whole process felt almost as creative as writing a poem from scratch.

Each participant approached the editorial process differently. Ben and Jenny were relatively tactful and reticent editors, treating this as an opportunity to re-shape poetic material in a different genre. Caroline Boon was the boldest of all of us, taking the greatest liberties with lineation, re-casting in prose, etc. She achieved some fascinating new effects. I think that with greater experience, over a wider range of examples, one might be able to discern an 'editorial identity' in each participant, comparable in many respects to their creative identity. Let me take two examples. It was noticeable to me, over the range of poems I edited, that I liked creating contrapuntal effects and using refrains. Also, that I disliked syntactical convolution, and preferred the plainest possible diction – this latter preference having an obvious genealogy in my interest in Wordsworth. Elizabeth Scott-Baumann, on the other hand, seemed most interested in enriching the tonal complexities of poems, and producing emotional shifts, through pauses or isolating words on the page.

If the intersection between our creative and critical identities was implicit in the way we edited the poems, it became sharpened in the kinds of notes we each appended to the edited texts. My own notes are very direct in their criticisms: this comes from my feeling greater confidence as a critic than as a poet. Lizzie's were less so; and it was obvious from the way she wrote them that she saw her editorial role as an enhancer, teasing out sub-textual meanings or thought patterns, rather than introducing new ones.

Some of us appreciated versions of our own poems which securely established their own separate identities (by being very different); but were less impressed by versions of our poems where minor alterations had been made. The psychology of this process would be well worth researching. My own hypothesis would be that writers feel a kind of proprietorial pride in their work; and don't always appreciate suggestions for improvement. A tinkered-with version makes its criticisms of the original overt. A wholly new version, on the other hand, elicits a new set of aesthetic responses and judgements. Offering itself up as an independent work of art, any critique it contains of the original is left implicit.

It would be interesting to see if some kind of consensus could be reached by a group about which editing has been most successful. When we compared our edited texts, I felt a surprisingly strong sense of which re-writing had worked, and which had not. Lizzie had re-written my sonnet very effectively, transforming the tension between octave and sestet into a tension that was there throughout, in a counterpointing of voices. This made it into an entirely new and *much better* poem. On the other hand, I felt that Caroline's and my own experiments with lineation had proved effective in some cases, but not all. In my view, this workshop demonstrated that editing, like translating, can involve the complete transformation of an art-work into something original, in which the voice of the editor/translator is as strong as (or stronger than) that of the original creator. But it also showed that, although all editing produces a new and different artwork, it does not follow that all editing is successful.

It would however be possible to reach different conclusions about what the editing process teaches us. The feminist poet Selima Hill has experimented with cutting poems and creating multiple versions, in which no final text is privileged. Experiments of this kind question where authority resides in a text, and whose authority establishes which text is considered to be final. Hill's questioning is underpinned by a belief in the equal validity of *all* forms of expression. According to this approach, the long swathes of poetry cut from *The Wasteland* are equal in aesthetic interest and merit to the published and canonised text. One editor's version of a poem is of equal value as another; what the editing process brings out is difference, not varying degrees of success.

The theoretical implications of editing are multifarious. It would be interesting to approach this activity *via* at least three different methodologies: 1) Using a Derridean approach to the editor's role, one might see her/him as a reader who 'deconstructs' the text. In this approach, the new poem is never more than merely provisional: the editor provides one line of many possible lines running through the parent poem, which keeps dissolving, to be re-composed in different forms with each new reading. 2) Using a Bakhtinian approach, one might consider the relation of 'monologic' to 'dialogic' discourse in the editing process. Assembling the numerous edited versions of a sonnet alongside the original, one begins to see the whole corpus as an intertextual collage of voices. The lyric voice of each individual writer (always monologic, in Mikhail Bakhtin's view), is here submerged in a polyphony of contending voices. 3) Using the kind of feminist poetics advocated by Mary Daly, one might consider editing as a species of dismantling, whose main purpose is to question patriarchal assumptions about the origins of language. Daly's methodology is Derridean, but she puts a feminist spin on deconstruction: 'In the beginning was not the word. In the beginning is the hearing. Spinsters spin deeper into the listening deep....We can weave and unweave, knot and unknot, only because we hear, what we hear, and as well as we hear'. Adapting her terminology, one might see the editor as a listener, who hears meanings not intended by the author and brings them within the hearing of others. To switch to a visual analogy, it is like turning a piece of embroidery over to see the pattern on the other side.

Whichever methodology one uses, there is an obvious question raised by the editing process. We can put this question formulaically: Who is the 'author' of *The Wasteland?*

Michel Foucault, in his ground-breaking essay 'What is an author?' argued that the concept of the author performs a classificatory function:

> The author is not an indefinite source of significations which fill a work; the author does not precede the works, he is a certain functional principle by which, in our culture, one limits, excludes, and chooses; in short, by which one impedes the free circulation, the free manipulation, the free composition, decomposition, and recomposition, of fiction.

It is interesting to think about how Foucault's definition of authorship applies to the poems in this book; and also what implications it has for the classificatory principles Jenny and I used in putting the book together. For instance, we were uncertain whether to arrange the edited texts alongside the originals, as though they were appendages or offshoots of it; or to place them in amongst the writings produced by each individual contributor to the volume. In an ideal world, the poems might appear in both places; but we opted for the former – partly, I think, because the workshop's editing had on the whole been fairly circumspect. However, in order to draw attention to the element of creativity in the editing process, we decided that the best way of attributing the poems was to place the editor in the position normally assigned to the author, but to follow that name with the author of the original text. Thus, Caroline Boon's version of Alice Wood's poem appears as 'Caroline Boon (after Alice Wood)'. That little word 'after' is very telling. It signals which text came first; and it also bespeaks disciple-ship; a certain obligation to be faithful to the original – to follow in the author's footsteps or listen to her spirit. However, in thinking about the implications of Foucault's analysis, I wonder if a more collaborative word might not be appropriate – especially given the workshop conditions under which all the texts in this volume were produced?

Conclusions

Throughout the workshop process, participants were involved in the dual process of creating and analysing. One or other of these activities may have been uppermost at any given moment, but their perpetual alternation meant that both sides were equally in play, and of equal importance. This gave all participants the opportunity to reflect on the relation between creativity and criticism. They were able to see the two activities as complementary, but also to notice the ways in which they came into creative tension. One obvious effect of all this was that it broke down hard and fast distinctions between the creative and the critical. We began to see them more as a continuum than as a dialectic. We noticed, for instance, how much our critical awareness came into play when we were writing – from the very earliest stages of selecting words for our poems, right through to producing a finished sonnet that fulfilled all the formal criteria. And, in the editing process particularly, we found that there was a possible synthesis of our creative and critical identities.

All this has interesting implications for the study of literary theory. Historically, criticism has played a secondary role in relation to literature. The rise of 'the critic' and professional criticism coincided with the rise of 'the author' – by which I mean the modern concept of the author, as someone who owns and is identified by name with his or her work. During the Romantic period and beyond, there has been a more or less explicit rivalry between creativity and criticism, with a steady increase in the status and authority accorded to critics. In the twentieth century, the importance of criticism was highlighted, first by the widespread acceptance of literature as a worthwhile object of study at university; and second by the advent of literary theory. Nowadays, theory is less fashionable than it was in the 1980's; but for a period of about twenty years, literary theorists accorded themselves an equivalent importance to creative writers. As the Yale critic Geoffrey Hartman once put it, 'Criticism is now crossing over into literature'.

In the academic teaching of English, the rise of criticism may have gone so far that it has blotted out a full understanding of what the creative process entails. Only by writing poetry themselves can students fully appreciate the choices and processes that are involved. By bringing creative and critical writing so closely into conjunction through our workshops, we were all able to experience at first hand what it was like to be at once 'primary' and 'secondary'. Through a kind of internal role-play, we could grasp the implications of the collaborative/competitive dynamic which always pertains between creation and reception; and which is peculiarly alive in poet/critics.

A final, more personal, conclusion. It was not until our final workshop that I realised how important it was to me that my students should talk about poetry *evaluatively*. So much of what we do in the academic study of English requires a studied neutrality where aesthetic tastes and judgements are concerned. We learn how to achieve a distance from ourselves in the act of critical reflection. We learn to put our personal tastes and ideological prejudices on one side, in order to achieve a historical awareness of the biography, politics, and aesthetic preferences of the author we are studying. We engage in scholarly research, so as to understand works of art in their original contexts. This painstakingly acquired objectivity gives us the ability to speak and write authoritatively about literature; but it does not help us to make evaluative judgements on our own behalves.

Before we can regard ourselves as critics, we need to become opinionated. As well as being able to say why a poem is written, under what circumstances, and for what purposes, we need to be confident in saying why it works.

Consolidating our aesthetic judgement involves analysing where our tastes come from, which interpretive community we identify with or belong to, and what literary fashions have influenced us. Acknowledging all these components in the formation of our taste makes us more articulate in defining and expressing it.

EVALUATIONS BY ALL PARTICIPANTS

Jenny Lewis

I came to these workshops from a background of more than 25 years of Creative Writing Teaching. My first training was with MIND where I ran workshops for three years at a drop-in centre for people with mental illness. As part of the training, I myself was required to have counselling, and this helped me to grasp that we are all part of the same continuum, albeit at different stages, and that qualitative judgements must be treated with caution. For example, how much do we dismiss or condemn something because we don't understand it? In one of my workshops, there was a schizophrenic who was capable of producing brilliant texts, each with its own architecture of logic. At the end of the day, the question had to be asked 'Where do we place this work and how do we view it as a piece of art?' The solution, often, was to class such work as 'therapeutic' which ducked the real issue. In the same way, many of my workshop participants were manic depressive. We have to ask, had Virginia Woolf been born a Harrogate housewife, could *To the Lighthouse* ever have been written?

I'm talking about an extreme situation, but as it is such an important context for my teaching practice, it should be mentioned. The St Edmund Hall group could be seen as the antithesis to the Harrogate group. These were bright young undergraduates, seen as the cream of the British university population, but the same principles came into play. Rather than teaching in a traditional, pedagogic way, Lucy and I were facilitating a flow of creative energy, stimulating thought, and sharing our knowledge of prosody. In their turn, the workshop members, by responding to stimuli and producing formal poems from the energy of the group dynamic, were completing a cycle. After each completed cycle, their confidence, knowledge of form and technique and ability to access creativity had improved. In this way, by group effort, each individual was taken gradually to a higher level throughout the duration of the workshops. The group, in fact, became the creator, but each person left the group with an enhanced level of competence.

Lucy and I had used the group dynamic in workshops before, but when this group first assembled, we wanted to try to monitor the processes more analytically. For this reason, we worked out with great care, in advance, how the group time would be structured. We also noted which members of the group seemed more or less confident, and whether there were those who needed extra affirmation to encourage them to reach their best potential. There was some suggestion, at the end of the process, that we had been too soft on ourselves. My answer is that, at this early stage, the crucial outcome is for each individual to grasp the value of his or her own potential as a creative writer. Without this self-belief, the writer will never be able to stay the course and withstand the batterings and buffetings of future teachers, reviewers and critics. To build a sense of one's own 'poetic self' – marking out psychological territories and finding a unified voice – is a slow and often painful process which goes on throughout the poet's life. To help people who are turning inwards to find this 'self' we need carrots rather than sticks to start with. The sticks come later. If we think that a Welsh Bard had to undergo a 12 year rigorous training, which involved long tracts of solitude and the ability to recite texts the length of the Bible by heart, before his or her talent was recognised, it puts the time-scale of poet-making into perspective.

After the first word association session, the group asked me if I would join them in the process of writing a sonnet. I was surprised by the level of my own resistance to this idea. While acting as a neutral facilitator, I felt sure of my ground and comfortable. I wasn't sure if I could retain the same degree of objectivity if I myself was writing poetry. This was the sensible, analytical reason. There was also a tremendous fear of failure, of being thought mediocre, of making a fool of myself in the group. This, I realised, was the challenge the rest of the group had been facing all along. I took a deep breath, wrote my sonnet and brought it to the workshop. I found that the act of reading my sonnet out became a sort of bonding ritual, and my relationship to the group became much closer after that. Through applying myself to the creative writing exercises along with the rest of the group, I found my own creative energies began to flow more spontaneously, and this has resulted in some of the best poetry I have written.

Lucy Newlyn

In terms of pedagogic practice, the most important finding of our experiment has been that tutors relate more authentically to students (and *vice versa*) when both are engaged in the same creative activity, giving it the same amount of energy, and reflecting on it together. What made the workshops so valuable was not so much the quality of the poetry they produced, as the quality of group activity they engendered. Like many small groups working together, this one experienced the satisfaction and excitement of achieving a communal identity. Contributing to the workshop was different from teaching or learning in tutorial or class; it was more like being involved in a dramatic production, a seminar, or a conference. More sense of shared community was as stake; personalities were openly engaged; less was held in reserve; greater risks were taken during discussion. As a result, the quality of intellectual exchange was higher. Not only did participants mostly come better prepared; they were all much more interested in what everyone had to say. This made discussion faster, more energetic and flowing, but also more focused.

The workshops were designed to demonstrate that the activities of creative writing and critical analysis are mutually enhancing. They clearly succeeded. On the critical front, we have observed in ourselves a greater awareness of form, and a greater ability to comment on it. This has come not just from increased practice in the use of technical terminology, but from the practical experience of writing to a particular specification. In addition, we have acquired a greater assurance and proficiency in making evaluative judgements about how well a writer achieves a desired effect and about what is good poetry. On the creative front, we have written some good poems, and achieved a sense of poetic identity in writing them. There has also been a spin-off for self-expression in a general sense. All participants have become more articulate in classes and tutorials, readier to take risks in expressing themselves. Furthermore, this enhanced sense of form is spilling over into the way we see the activity of writing essays. Students are paying more attention to the construction of their arguments, to the length and shape of their sentences; and to how their prose sounds when read aloud. All this has come from seeing essays as *analogous* to poems.

Ben Burton

Using creative writing as a means of exploring literary theory has proven to be a rewarding and enjoyable experience. The workshops encouraged students to respond to questions concerning poetic form, literary theory and the editorial process in an imaginative and personal way. This experience removes the traditional hierarchical relationship between tutor and student, creating an environment in which ideas can be exchanged with confidence and passion. I have particularly enjoyed the combined activity of writing poetry and commentaries on other students' work. This has not only introduced me to the pleasure of creative writing, but has also prompted me to consider the process of critical analysis more thoroughly. Through composing and editing my own poetry, I feel more sensitive to the range of decisions poets make, whether consciously or not, as they write. The poetry workshops have also provided me with a way of enjoying and familiarising myself with prominent subjects in literary theory such as authorship, form, rhyme-analysis and editing. By discussing these matters in the context of my own creative writing, I have been attracted to elements of my English degree that might otherwise have seemed 'dry' and 'abstract'.

Caroline Boon

The poetry workshops have inspired my creative side whilst helping me to understand the nuances of poetry much better. Initially I found it hard to compose my own poetry, awestruck by the brilliance of the canon, which confronts us daily in our academic work. The workshops however, stimulated creative thinking and encouraged new ways of examining popular poetical themes. The process of discussion and revision of our own and each other's poetry prompted a clearer understanding of the poetical process and a real investigation into the concept of authorial intention. Consequently, I find I have begun to examine language much more closely. In my academic work I now consider the implications of what I write in ways which just would not have occurred to me without the classes. On an entirely practical note, I was also able to write a finals paper on 'Rhythm and Metre' with much more confidence than I would have had previously. Finally, I think an important part of any education is to inspire. The creative nature of the poetry classes encourages one to approach common concepts and modes of thought in new and innovative ways, which is invaluable to any student, whatever career or interest they choose to pursue in the future.

Brendan Jones

I felt that the St Edmund Hall poetry workshop worked best when it treated writing as a process and a practice. Creative fingerprints of each of the participants, owing to particular background and personal experience, were respected and given scope through an insistence on using certain forms, such as the sonnet. The workshop also emphasised the art of creation and revision, while simultaneously encouraging students to keep their pens moving through spontaneous writing exercises. The workshop was also successful in disrupting the dualism of tutor/student that is the pedagogical norm at Oxford. This made for an atmosphere that was much more conducive to writing. There was a horizontality to the class which was a relief from the everyday dynamics between students and tutors found in the university.

I thought that peer criticism could have been more honest. I understand that remarks must be treated with great care, as too much criticism given at the wrong moment can dampen the creative spark. Nevertheless, I think that, once a trust is developed among participants, once the class becomes a secure and supportive place, the gloves should be taken off, as everyone attends to become a better writer. There were times when participants, including myself, could have been more up-front when it came to taking apart certain lines written by participants. In the most successful workshops, a balance is struck between encouraging students to write and providing them with useful critical feedback. I felt that there was too much of the former.

I thought that the workshop's most important accomplishment was that it provided an alternative model of learning. This is much more the 'round table' approach, characterised by there being no privileged voice. The group, when it moved forward most effectively – for example, in the sonnets taking form out of words spontaneously written during class – functioned very much like a vessel with disparate fragments coming together to make a whole. However, this strength turned into a fault when participants refused to react strongly to a piece of writing for fear of fragmenting this same group. I think that it is only the continual process of destruction and renewal which makes both for good writing, and for a good writing workshop.

Elizabeth Scott-Baumann

For me one of the most important effects of the poetry workshop was that I was forced (perhaps I should say forced myself) to produce poetry in a specific form, and on a specified subject. The prospect of placing reluctantly written work before a critical, and highly respected, audience, was enough to produce initially implacable writer's block! However, the challenge of writing and of exploring poetic form on both a creative and an analytical level almost simultaneously, proved highly rewarding. The sequence of brainstorming-writing-analysing forced me to probe the skills used in my English literature degree. The analytical path "what was the author thinking?" followed so often (and often fruitlessly) was valuably forced into question in a context where each individual was both poet and critic, and the chiasmic actions of creating and deconstructing became parts of the same process.

The poetry workshop was enlightening as much in its critical element as in the creative element. I found myself forced to engage in the critical debate over the level of importance that should be attributed to biographical information in analysing texts. As a fairly close-knit group, socially as well as academically, we could often identify the factual source of the experiences and emotions expressed in each other's poetry. Knowing the biographical facts behind the poetry, having emotional attachments within the group, and analysing the poetry in the presence of the poets complicated the process of critical analysis, and forced each one of us, I think, to examine our techniques. I found myself consciously trying to exclude personal knowledge of the poet when analysing his/her work. The workshop forced me to objectify my critical analysis skills in the very context in which I could be most subjective.

Alice Wood

It was very productive to meet in a group both to write and comment upon poetry. The atmosphere created in the group by the process of writing collectively made it easy to discuss each other's work openly. It was helpful that nothing was taken too seriously, although what started as simply playing around with words and rhythms would often lead to something genuinely productive. I feel I have gained a lot more confidence in both my creative writing and my critical skills because of this relaxed atmosphere. I think all of us also found a lot of inspiration through hearing other people's work and through hearing feedback on our own work. I particularly gained a lot of inspiration through learning about poetic form from others, and this has also aided my appreciation of poetry. By increasing my knowledge of poetic form and also by increasing my confidence in my ability to interpret poetry, I feel these workshops may have quite substantially improved my performance in the critical commentary paper of our first year exams.

Synergy between Teaching and Learning: Does *Synergies* challenge the traditional separation of teaching and learning?

Paul Ashwin
Institute for Advancement of University Learning,
University of Oxford

There are many interesting educational aspects to the fascinating experiment that is outlined in the rest of this book. Many of these have been examined in some detail in earlier contributions. These include the potential for students' engagement in the St Edmund Hall Poetry Workshop to impact on their communication and creativity and their approaches to, and understanding of, their academic work. However, there is another aspect that I am interested in examining. In her reflections on the process, Lucy stresses the importance of the tutors and the students engaging in the same creative activity (p.87) and Brendan saw the workshop as 'disrupting the dualism of tutor/student that is the pedagogical norm at Oxford' and offering "an alternative model of learning" (p.89). It is the issue raised by these two reflections that my contribution will focus on, as the aspect of the experiment that interests me most is whether *Synergies* represents a challenge to the traditional separation between teaching and learning.

I have argued elsewhere that traditional approaches to teaching and learning tend to view teaching and learning as two different processes (Ashwin 2003). To put it very simply, teaching is often thought to be what the teacher or tutor does, whilst learning is thought to be what the learner or student does. This division can hinder students' learning if they or their tutors overly focus on the students' or the tutor's responsibility for teaching and learning situations, rather than seeing that tutors and students have a joint responsibility for ensuring that teaching and learning situations are as productive as possible. In the experiment described in this book an alternative approach to the traditional separation of teaching and learning was adopted. Teaching and learning were conceived as parts of a single process. All those involved in the poetry workshop were engaged in a joint enterprise, for which all were responsible. They wrote collaboratively and then both tutors and students wrote original poems, which were critiqued and edited by tutors and students alike. This is very different from the situation these students describe experiencing in tutorials, in which the student produces an essay that the tutor then critiques. This is not to say that in this experiment the roles of teachers and learners were identical; it was the tutors who decided, for example, the subject and form of the poetry, and the structure of activities. However, within this structure the tutors and the students were engaged in joint production of poetry. Whilst there are other models and examples in Higher Education where the responsibility for aspects of the teaching and learning process has been given to students (for example see Abercrombie 1960, Eraut et al 1975, Heron 1989, Rowland 1993), these have not focused on what happens when tutors and students are engaged in the same task.

The view of teaching and learning adopted in this book is consistent with Lave and Wenger's (1991) theory of learning as legitimate peripheral participation. This theory illuminates an alternative way of approaching the teaching and learning process that does not separate teaching and learning. For Lave and Wenger learning involves becoming increasing involved in the practice of an expert, as is the case in apprenticeship. Their argument, which is based on studies of successful apprentice/master relations in contexts as diverse as Goan tailors and reforming alcoholics, is summarised by Hanks (1991):

> The apprentice's ability to understand the master's performance depends not on their possessing the same representations of it, but rather on their engaging in the performance in congruent ways. Similarly, the master's effectiveness at producing learning is not dependent on her ability to inculcate the student with her own conceptual representations. Rather, it depends on her ability to manage effectively a division of participation that provides for growth on the part of the student. (p.21)

However, all this is, at most, a potentially elegant description of a process that *may* have occurred in the workshop, with Jenny and Lucy, as tutors, managing a division of participation that allowed the students involved to grow. There are many beautifully described ideas in the literature on teaching and learning in Higher Education that when examined in more detail do not seem to live up to their description. How can we go beyond this description to get a better sense of what may have happened in, and as a result of, the students' and tutors' involvement in this poetry workshop? One approach, which I shall attempt here, is to make a series of hypotheses about what one might expect to happen if students and tutors were engaged in the process in a way that is described above and then examine the available evidence to see if that fits with these hypotheses.

So what might one expect to happen if students and tutors were engaged in a single task in writing, critiquing, and editing original poetry? First, this would represent a change in the roles of tutors and students and so one would expect some discussion of this and some attempt to think about how they might transfer this changed view of the roles of students' and tutors' into other teaching and learning interactions. Second, as the roles of teachers and learners become less separated, one might expect students to have an increased sense of academic community, as they perceive that they are gaining access to the community of which their tutors are a part. Again, one would expect some discussion of how this might be transferred into other teaching and learning interactions. Finally, one would expect tutors to describe their learning from the process in a way that is similar to the students. If tutors were to get very different things out of the process than students then we might question whether they were actually involved in the same process as the students and ask whether they were instead engaged in a different process.

My responses to these hypotheses are based upon a group discussion that I facilitated with the tutors and five of the students involved in the project. This discussion took place straight after the session in which the group had discussed their editing of each other's poems. I first asked the group to reflect on what had happened in that session and we used this as a starting point to discuss what the group saw as the critical aspects of the poetry workshop as well as how they had benefited from them. The comments I make in my contribution are based on the observations made by the group in this discussion and are illustrated by student and, in one case, tutor quotations. To preserve student anonymity, I have not assigned these quotations to particular students. This account clearly offers only one point of view of the process at one particular time. I invite others to examine the rest of this book and think about other potential viewpoints.

Hypothesis 1: A change in roles of teachers and learners

The students did appear to perceive a change in the roles of tutors and students within this process compared to their experience of other teaching and learning interactions. This seemed to be related to the students' perceptions that they and the tutors were all engaged in a single task.

> I think it was really important that you [the tutors] both participated in the same way that we all have in that you come to it with slightly different perspective because we're students and you're a tutor but I think it's really important that you've both been writing poems from the same formula that we are and taking the same words away. I think it's just the idea that a tutor becomes a partner in learning rather than sort of guardian of learning.

This contrasted with students' experiences in tutorials where they felt they were the ones who were producing work for the tutor to comment on.

> The [poetry workshop] made me realise that an essay for me is just as much a form of personal expression as doing a poem is. It's just as much me putting my heart on the line about how I feel about something and how I care about something and if other people are doing that at the same time, that 'baring-all' kind of thing, it doesn't feel as [much of] a risk. In some ways in a tutorial you spend a week or whatever putting your all into something and really caring very deeply about it, thinking about it but sometimes the fact that you're the only one who's done that [in the tutorial relationship] can feel quite difficult.

This perception that the tutors and students were both engaged in the same process was accompanied by a perception that there was less of a directive relationship between the students and the tutors within the workshop compared to tutorials:

> I think that says something about the group and the dynamics of the group. I think it doesn't seem like if you [the tutor] suggested something then we have to bow down to your authority because you've organised the classes and because you've been teaching literature. I think generally there has been like more of a levelling kind of process as the classes have gone on.
>
> The regular model [in tutorials] is there's somebody in this big armchair and then you have your little chair and he has some sort of, or she has some sort of, monopoly on truth and that's how it happens and you can try and subvert that truth but once you do he's going very quickly, she's very quickly going to, try and put you in line.

There was also evidence that the students had thought about how they might transfer elements of this experience into the tutorial setting. There was some discussion about whether the experience of the different roles in the poetry workshop was transferred only into their tutorials with the *same* tutor as in the workshop (i.e. Lucy) or whether there were general benefits in students' experiences of different tutor and student relationships. Some felt the latter was the case:

> It's a bridge - you've built one relationship with a tutor in one way so then when you go to a new tutor you immediately start from a completely different level to where you did when you were in your first year and you were in the first term and you walked into your tutor's room and sat down and there was a spectre of your tutor on her big bear chair and there were you on your baby bear chair. You've got [the workshop] as a bridge acting between the two, so it's not just about building relationships with one tutor, it's to do with self-confidence and how you see yourself and how you know yourself, you then immediately kind of transpose that relationship on to it for a new relationship with a new tutor.

Another student did not experience a change in the relationship they had with their tutors outside of the workshop. This student suggested that, whilst the workshop had offered the potential for there to be a new kind of relationship between tutor and student as a result of the workshop, this depended on the tutor being willing to accept this new kind of tutorial relationship.

> I've realised it does come to depend on how much the tutor is willing to allow that change to take place and no matter how much you might want to be on more of an equal basis, some tutors may actually like having that hierarchy kind of thing.

However, whether students were successful in transferring the relationship between tutor and student that they experienced in the workshop into the tutorials, there does seem to be some quite strong evidence that they did perceive the relationship between tutors and students in the workshop as different from the previous experience of teaching and learning interactions at Oxford; and that they did *attempt* to use their understanding of this changed relationship in a different teaching and learning situation.

Hypothesis 2: An increased sense of academic community

Some of the students suggested that the experiences of the group process in the workshop had enabled them to experience a different form of communication within an academic setting, one which was based more on the group building on each other's ideas rather than confrontational argument. As hypothesised, this appeared to engender a heightened sense of academic community:

> I think that would really point to the effectiveness of the course because it seemed to be very important within an academic context where you really don't get a lot of listening or a lot of community discussion where people actually listen to what other people are saying, incorporate it into their own work and then come back with a response whether it be in the form of a poem or comment. I found in an academic setting it's much more confrontational and adversarial and I think that just providing that different model of communication within the world of academe has been beneficial.

For one student, this sense of community appeared to be enhanced by the feeling that the college had offered the opportunity of having some work published:

> One of the things that made me feel something about the University that I hadn't felt before, was that I was being encouraged to do something that meant a lot to me. I wanted to do some writing and the college had given me an opportunity where I could do that and

> enable me to publish something in a collection of poems and enabled me to do a really important thing that meant something to me.

Again there was evidence that the students attempted to transfer this sense of community into their view of tutorials.

> One thing it's made me feel is that people who are here are passionate about this subject, not necessarily about writing poetry but about English, and recognising that the person who's in a tutorial with you is passionate about it and that your tutor is passionate about it has actually made that part of the community feel of tutorials for me. We all feel very deeply about what we're doing, it's not just a kind of dry exercise where we're all going through the motions.

Thus, for some of the students involved, the workshop did appear to increase their sense of academic community. This did not come out as strongly in the discussion as the students' perception that they had experienced a different relationship between tutors and students. One possible explanation for this is that those students who had successfully transferred this new relationship into their tutorials with other tutors (i.e. tutors not involved in the experiment) were more likely to experience an increased sense of academic community. For the others, whilst they clearly valued the sense of the community in the workshop, it is possible that once outside of the workshop they felt that this increased sense of community was blocked by tutors who "may actually like having that hierarchy kind of thing".

Hypothesis 3: Tutor learning

The final hypothesis focused on the processes of the tutors' learning. As the earlier contributions by Jenny and Lucy in this book illustrate, they did appear to learn in similar ways to the students. They didn't necessarily learn the *same things*, but then again nor did the students all learn the same things as each other, but their learning was of the *same type* as the students. For example, in the group discussion Jenny disclosed:

> I wasn't writing when we started doing this . . . and when we came to write the sonnets, the group asked me if I would join in and I was very resistant actually. I thought 'I don't want to do this, it's hard

> work, I'm putting myself on the line, I'm supposed to be a poet and they will judge me and I will lose credibility' but I'm so glad I did because I've actually found a new way of writing through it because, in another workshop, I actually wrote a poem that was completely different from my normal way of writing. So I feel it's been enormously beneficial to me this just being a part of the group . . . I had a breakthrough. It wouldn't have happened unless I'd been with the group, had to produce something and had forced myself to go and work on it, think about it, write it and then type it up and bring it to the class. It was a huge breakthrough.

Conclusion

There appears to be evidence to support the hypotheses that were made earlier and thus to support the earlier description of *Synergies* as a project in which teaching and learning were conceived as a single process, and the roles of tutor and student were not separated in a way that is traditional within teaching and learning situations. However, the account given here, being based on a group discussion of the students and tutors, is partial and one in which some factors are probably under emphasised or hidden. Equally, I would not want to suggest that this experiment could be easily transferred into other contexts, as there are a number of factors that are likely to have affected the way the experiment played out in practice.

A factor that was largely hidden in my discussion with tutors and students was how power operated within the group. Some of the students talked about how they were 'cajoled' into joining the workshop but they appeared to view this as a use of power that had positive consequences:

> I think it is really important that we were quite cajoled into it because I would never have come to a poetry class before, I just wouldn't. Even if it had been plastered all over college, advertised everywhere you went . . . I just wouldn't have gone. I hadn't written a poem before we had to for you [Lucy and Jenny] since kind of primary school. It would just have been 'well that's not really my thing' and it is totally my thing now I've done it but I just wouldn't have done it.

There are probably other issues of power that were not visible within the discussion between the tutors and students. These were perhaps represented when students talked tentatively of their feelings about critiquing the tutors' poems. Issues of power were also suggested in the way that the discussion focused on the collaborative learning of the group but not on whether the group had taught collaboratively; this still appeared to be an activity that was the reserve of the tutors. However, there are always going to be issues of power in group work. The students' and tutors' accounts suggest a group of people working hard to keep a group process as productive as possible and that this was made possible by the fact that they were all engaged in the process of developing collaborative, as well as their own, original work.

The first factor that is likely to have affected the way the experiment played out in practice is that it took place in the context of St Edmund Hall and the University of Oxford. It is clear that the tutorial process acted as a reference point for students when they were thinking about their experiences in the poetry workshop and it seems probable that if the students had used other forms of teaching and learning interactions as their reference point then their reflections would have been different. Secondly, as part of the context of St Edmund Hall, some of the students had previous experience of contributing to a collaborative project that led to the production of the St Edmund Hall poetry anthology *Chatter of Choughs*, which they knew from the outset would result in a published work. This is likely to have encouraged the sustained involvement in the process. Thirdly, the students' relationship with Lucy before they became involved in the workshop, and with Lucy and Jenny once they became involved in the workshop, appears to have been a critical factor in making the workshop a success. Finally, the way in which the group bonded and the commitment that each participant demonstrated by completing the work that they had agreed to do seemed to be critical to the tutors and students developing a sense of academic community.

Despite these cautionary notes, this experiment does appear to have adopted an alternative to the traditional way of approaching teaching and learning situations: one in which, instead of teaching and learning being separated between the roles of tutor and student, students and tutors learnt together through their engagement in a single task. This appears to have enabled those involved to see the role of tutors and students in a different way and to have led to an enhanced sense of academic community in which tutors and students learned together. Whilst this experiment could not be directly transferred into other contexts, this book as a whole offers a resource that others can use in conducting their own experiments and in doing so find ways congruent with their contexts in which they can challenge the traditional divide between teaching and learning.

References:

Abercrombie, M.L.J (1960) *The Anatomy of Judgement : An investigation into the processes of perception and reasoning* (London, Hutchinson).

Ashwin, P. (2003) Peer facilitation and how it contributes to the development of a more social view of learning. *Research in Post-Compulsory Education 8(1).*

Eraut, M., MacKenzie, N. and Papps, I. (1975) 'The mythology of educational development: reflections on a three-year study of economics teaching'. *British Journal of Educational Technology,* 6(3), pp.20-34.

Hanks, W.F (1991) 'Foreword' in Lave, J. and Wenger, E. (1991) *Situated Learning: Legitimate Peripheral Participation.* (Cambridge, Cambridge University Press).

Heron, J. (1989) *The Facilitator's Handbook* (London, Kogan Page).

Lave, J. and Wenger, E. (1991) *Situated Learning: Legitimate Peripheral Participation.* (Cambridge, Cambridge University Press).

Rowland, S (1993) *The Enquiring Tutor: Exploring the Process of Professional Learning* (London, Falmer Press).